A Dialogue with Nature

Romantic Landscapes from Britain and Germany

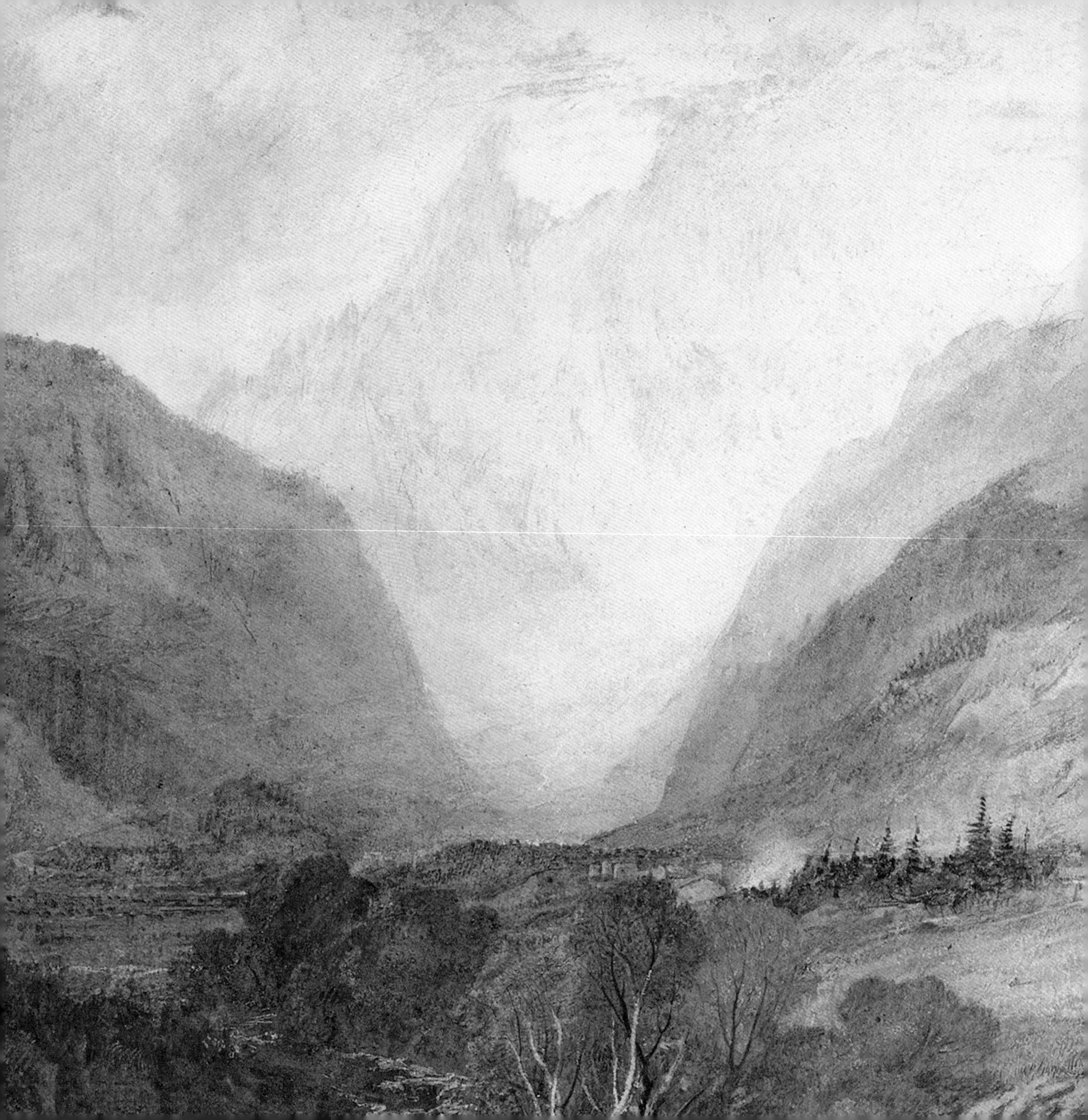

A Dialogue with Nature

Romantic Landscapes from Britain and Germany

Matthew Hargraves and Rachel Sloan

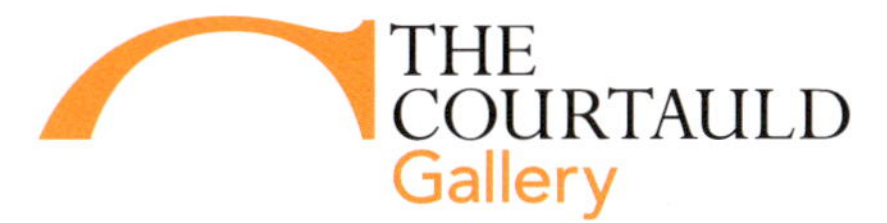

First published to accompany the exhibition

*A Dialogue with Nature: Romantic
Landscapes from Britain and Germany*

The Courtauld Gallery, London, 30 January – 27 April 2014
The Morgan Library & Museum, New York, 30 May – 7 September 2014

The Courtauld Gallery is supported by the
Higher Education Funding Council for England (HEFCE)

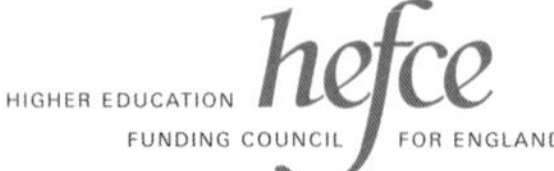

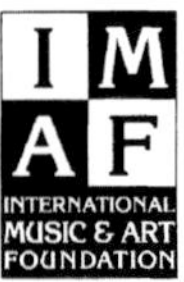

Copyright © 2014
Text copyright © the authors
Images copyright © The Samuel Courtauld Trust, The Courtauld
Gallery, London, and © The Morgan Library & Museum, New York

ISBN 978 1 907372 66 7

British Library Cataloguing in Publication Data
A catalogue record for this book is available from the British Library

Produced by Paul Holberton publishing
89 Borough High Street, London SE1 1NL
www.paul-holberton.net

Designed by Laura Parker
www.parkerinc.co.uk

Origination and printing by
E-graphic, Verona, Italy

FRONT COVER Fohr, *The Ruins of Hohenbaden*, cat. 13 (detail)
FRONT FLAP Constable, *Cloud Study*, cat. 9 (detail)
BACK COVER Cozens, *A ruined fort near Salerno*, cat. 14 (detail)
BACK FLAP von Dillis, *Cloud Study*, cat. 7 (detail)

Contents

Acknowledgements

This exhibition, the first collaboration between the Courtauld Gallery and the Morgan Library & Museum, would not have been possible without the support and advice of many individuals and institutions. We are especially grateful to Ernst Vegelin van Claerbergen and Stephanie Buck at the Courtauld and to William Griswold, Linda Wolk-Simon and Jennifer Tonkovich at the Morgan for the opportunity to curate the exhibition and for their help and encouragement at all stages. We would also like to thank Edward Payne and Per Rumberg for their support and enthusiasm for the project; conservators Kate Edmondson and Lindsey Tyne for sharing their expertise on drawing media; and Julia Blanks and John Alexander for their exemplary organisation of the exhibition's logistics. Karin Kyburz and Marilyn Palmeri provided invaluable assistance with the catalogue images. We are also grateful to Jonathan Harrison and Mary Nixon of the Senate House Library at the University of London for their generous loan of the volume of *The Works of Lord Byron* containing the engraving after Turner's watercolour *Cologne* in the Courtauld's collection.

For their assistance with the writing of the catalogue entries, we would like to thank Susan Owens (guest curator at the Courtauld Gallery in 2012), Ann Gunn, Anne Lyles, Jane Roberts, Joanna Selborne, Greg Smith and Timothy Wilcox. We are also indebted to all those who offered welcome encouragement and generously shared their knowledge, especially Graeme Barraclough, Louisa Dare, Gillian Forrester, Sarah Green, Henrietta Hine, Paul Holberton, Elizabeth Jacklin, Jack Kettlewell, Emily Leonardo, Chloe Le Tissier, Colin Lindley, Caireen McGinn, Belinda Moore, Laura Parker, David Solkin, and Hannah Talbot.

Finally, we would like to express our deep gratitude to Lowell Libson, who generously supported Matthew Hargraves's fellowship at the Morgan Library's Drawings Institute which made possible this collaboration between two great collections of drawings, and to the International Music and Art Foundation for supporting the exhibition and the continuing study, conservation and display of drawings at the Courtauld Gallery.

Matthew Hargraves, Yale Center for British Art
Rachel Sloan, The Courtauld Gallery

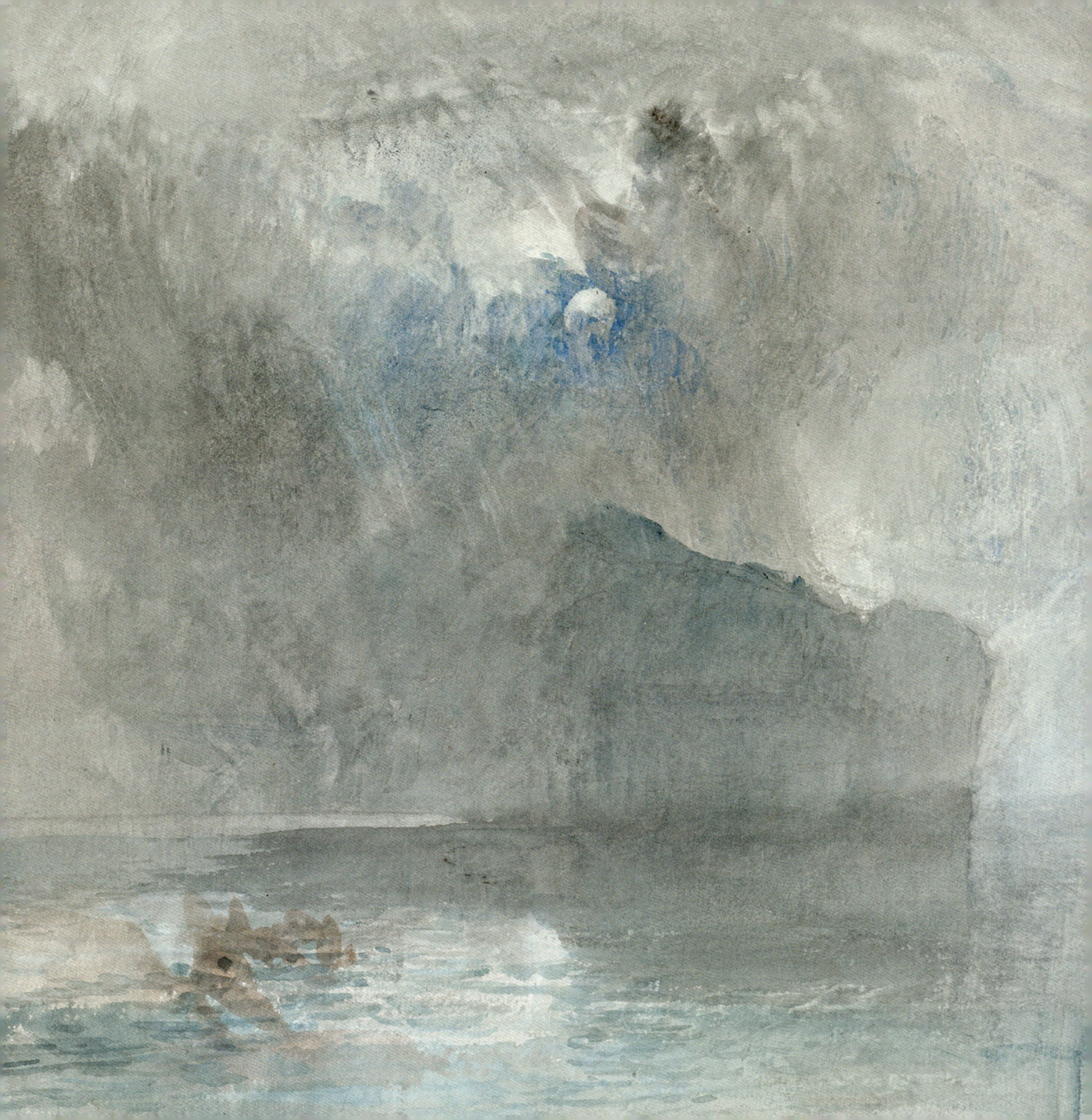

Foreword

This exhibition brings together holdings from The Morgan Library & Museum, which cares for one of the finest collections of drawings in the world, and the Courtauld Gallery which, as part of the Courtauld Institute of Art, is one the world's leading university art museums.

The collecting, scholarly research and public display of drawings is fundamental to both our institutions and is animated by a deeper understanding of drawings as embedded in the history of ideas and thought. This broad approach informed two important recent developments in London and New York. In 2010 a major grant from the International Music and Art Foundation enabled the Courtauld Gallery to create its IMAF Centre for Drawings. The following year the Morgan Library & Museum established the Drawing Institute through the generosity of Eugene V. Thaw. These complementary initiatives are committed to deepening research and stimulating new approaches to the study of drawings. Both also embrace the possibilities of collaboration and it seemed self-evident from the start that the Morgan and the Courtauld should work together. Alongside informal collaboration, this led to the establishment of a Morgan-Courtauld fellowship and a commitment to a distinctive programme of small jointly-organised exhibitions.

Exhibitions often come with great costs and matching expectations, conditions which can have an inhibiting effect on creativity and curiosity. In shaping our programme we wished to consider the virtues of a more modest approach. Drawn from our two collections, our occasional exhibitions will be relatively small in scale and open and exploratory in character. Rather than attempting definitive statements they will seek to encourage discussion and stimulate ideas.

A Dialogue with Nature is a fitting first chapter in our collaboration. Selected principally from the Morgan's exceptional group of German drawings and the Courtauld's wide-ranging British holdings it reflects on artists' changing relationship with nature and the landscape during the Romantic period. There are relatively few opportunities for audiences to see British and German works of this era side by side, and this display was conceived as offering the opportunity to consider points of commonality as well as divergence.

We were especially fortunate to have Matthew Hargraves of the Yale Center for British Art as the first Morgan-Courtauld Fellow. Matthew worked closely on the project with Rachel Sloan, his co-curator at the Courtauld. We thank them both for embracing the spirit of this partnership and for so successfully inaugurating our joint programme.

At the Morgan this project is made possible, in part, by the Rita Markus Fund for Exhibitions and a generous gift from Lowell Libson Ltd. The Courtauld wishes to thank the International Music and Art Foundation. Valuable support was also provided by the International Partners Charity Fund, in memory of Melvin R. Seiden.

Ernst Vegelin van Claerbergen
HEAD OF THE COURTAULD GALLERY

William M. Griswold
DIRECTOR, THE MORGAN LIBRARY & MUSEUM

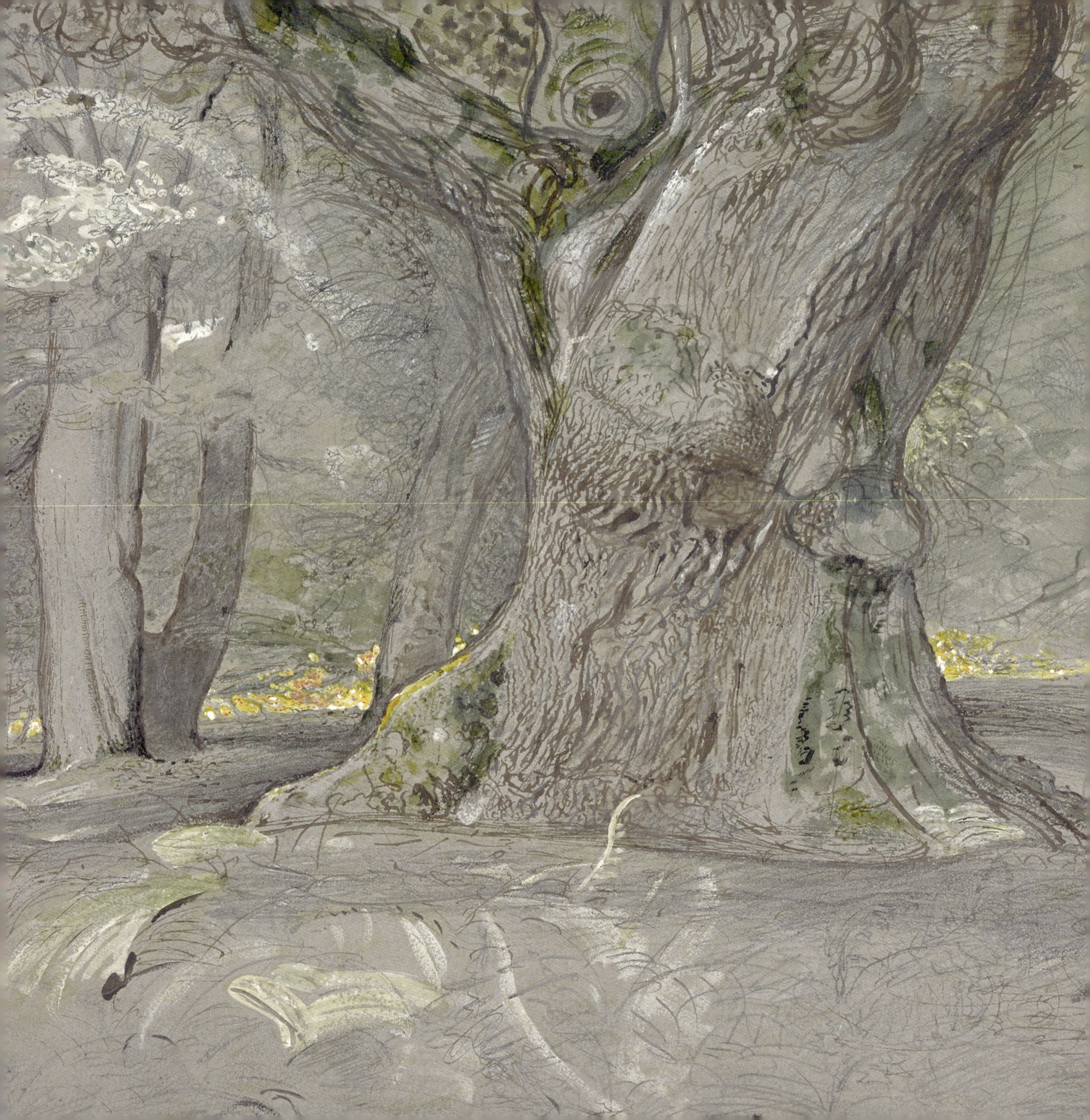

Introduction

MATTHEW HARGRAVES

An Age of Revolutions

At the close of the eighteenth century, while wars and revolutions rocked Europe, landscape art began a quiet transformation. With the rise of industrialization, capitalism and urbanization, the very meaning and value of land itself was thrown into question as centuries of what seemed like unchangeable order were brought swiftly to a close. The map of continental Europe was redrawn as the armies of Revolutionary France moved on to the offensive with dramatic success. The Napoleonic age saw the occupation of the German lands, the suppression of principalities and republics, the end of the Holy Roman Empire, and the creation of new kingdoms and dependencies. Britain was blockaded and feared invasion at least until the defeat of the French and its allied navies at Trafalgar in 1805, and thereafter spent almost a decade at war in the Iberian Peninsula to contain Napoleon's ambition to dominate Europe. As political geography was shifting, so approaches to landscape underwent profound change. British and German artists were in the vanguard when forging a new visual vocabulary in what Caspar David Friedrich called a "dialogue with nature".[1]

Before Romanticism

In 1809 the German Friedrich Wilhelm Basilius, Baron von Ramdohr published a broadside against "that mysticism that is now slinking in everywhere and that wafts towards us from art and science, from philosophy and religion, like a narcotic vapour".[2] His specific target was Friedrich's *Cross in the Mountains*, a landscape painting installed as an altarpiece in the castle chapel at Tetschen for his patron Countess Maria Theresa von Thun und Hohenstein. His more general target, however, was the new sensibility in art and literature that rejected the systems and certainties of the Enlightenment.

Conventional aesthetics held that landscape art dealt with either common nature or ideal nature, the former mode being exemplified by the Dutch tradition of describing nature, the latter having its apogee in the idealized, narrative landscapes of Claude.[3] Moreover, landscape art could never be a substitute for history painting since it belonged among the subordinate genres, the purpose of which was primarily to please by evoking sentiments, unlike exalted history painting which existed to instruct. Within landscape art, the ideal was considered superior to the descriptive and, for Ramdohr's generation, the defining landscape drawings were those in Claude's *Liber Veritatis* in the collection of the Duke of Devonshire in London, which were reproduced in mezzotint and disseminated across Europe by Richard Earlom in the 1770s. Goethe himself praised Claude in the following terms: ". . . his pictures are true, yet have no trace of actuality. Claude Lorrain knew the real world by heart, down to the minutest details, but he used it only as the means of expressing the world of his beautiful soul. This is the true ideal."[4] It was this tradition that predominated in both Britain and Germany before the narcotic vapour of Romanticism began to spread in Dresden and London. The work of Johann Georg Wagner working in Dresden a generation before Friedrich is characteristic of what Ramdohr had in mind – drawings and etchings of bucolic rural life, of shepherds and goatherds, milkmaids and their cattle in benign countryside. In Britain a close parallel can be found in Gainsborough's idyllic drawings of rural industry or rustic leisure, typically made indoors from the imagination or from models set up on a table-top. Both artists took as their starting point a notion of a lost golden age of ideal nature now only glimpsed beneath the accidents of the corrupted world.

Poetry and Truth

In 1782 two artists, the German Jakob Philipp Hackert and the British John Robert Cozens, met in Naples; both would change the course of landscape art in their respective countries. Hackert, originally from Berlin, arrived in Rome in 1768 and remained in Italy for the rest of his life. While continuing to revere the art of Claude, Hackert became interested in working directly from nature, something Claude was said to have done but was then only gradually coming back into vogue. Recalling his own visit to Rome in 1770, his friend Goethe claimed that the example of the German brothers Philipp and Georg Hackert shocked other artists: "In Rome, at that time, it was unusual to draw from nature . . . least of all did one consider sketching and finishing a fairly large drawing from nature. The French *pensionnaires* were all amazed when they saw the two Hackerts roaming the countryside with large portfolios, executing finished outline drawings in pen and ink or, indeed, highly finished watercolors and even paintings entirely from nature." This desire to ground landscape art in the direct study of particular nature became

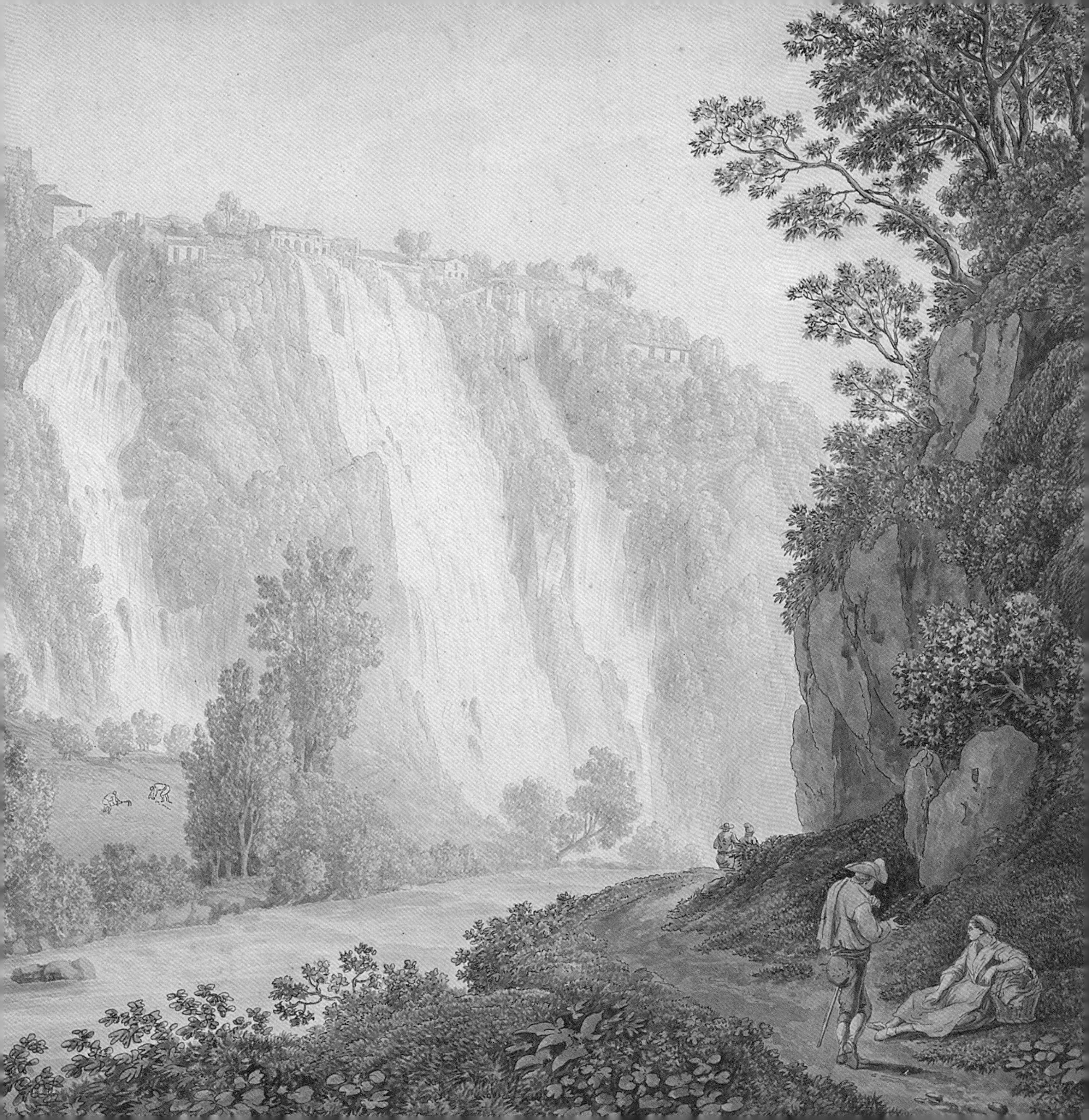

characteristic of the Romantic sensibility, but Goethe still distinguished Hackert's drawings from landscape art proper which he continued to maintain consisted of scenes of ideal nature in a Claudean manner.[5] Instead Hackert was producing 'views' or 'illustrations' of remarkable fidelity and detail, yet lifted from the merely descriptive by an idealizing approach. Hackert was familiar to British artists in Italy. Thomas Jones noted his "minute finishing" but felt that "most German artists . . . study more the *Minutiae* than the grand principles of the Art".[6] When Hackert met John Robert Cozens in Naples, Cozens was on his second Italian tour making views from nature in the service of William Beckford.[7] Unlike the sharp linearity of Hackert's style, Cozens's topographical drawings for Beckford introduced an entirely new sophistication and sensibility into watercolour through an unmatched richness of colour along with a new depth and consistency of tone, giving his landscapes a unity that was lacking in the work of earlier artists. His ruined fort at Salerno has none of the minutiae of Hackert or that would characterize German Romantic draughtsmanship, and is instead infused with an unmistakable melancholy that produces an emotional and subjective response akin to that "narcotic vapour" that so troubled Ramdohr about Friedrich, but which John Constable admired as "all poetry".[8] While taking different approaches, both Hackert and Cozens were transforming perceptions about what landscape art should be, or could aspire to achieve.

The School of Nature

The new engagement with working outdoors found in Hackert peaked in the first decades of the nineteenth century in Britain and Germany. Constable, who praised Cozens as "the greatest genius that ever touched landscape", famously turned his attention to skies, working on a series of cloud studies in oil around 1820 when living in Hampstead. Artists across Europe were also studying the fleeting effects of clouds, their instability and resistance to tidy narrative being among their appeals. In Munich, Johann Georg von Dillis produced almost 150 cloud studies in white chalk on blue paper in the first two decades of the nineteenth century when working for Ludwig I of Bavaria. His remarkable body of drawings and oil sketches on paper from nature reflect an affinity for his British counterparts and the fact that of all German landscape painters he was the best acquainted with British trends.[9] The painterly qualities in Dillis's sketches – his willingness to move away from austere linearity – mark him out among his German contemporaries, but these traits rarely found their way into his finished landscapes, which remained idealizing in approach, for both Constable and Dillis encountered opposition. Sir George Beaumont famously argued that Constable's landscapes were too green, and lacked the venerable brown tint of the Old Masters and a solid grounding in tradition.[10] Dillis was forced to follow conventional taste in his finished work and even witnessed a reaction against the burgeoning of landscape art from the triumph of German history painting led by the Nazarenes in Rome. When the leading Nazarene Peter Cornelius settled in Munich in 1826 he suppressed the existing professorship of landscape in the Academy there.[11] By then, the reputation of the ageing Hackert had long been eclipsed by the Austrian Josef Anton Koch, whose heroic landscapes blended careful observation of mountainous nature with Claudean idealization and an austere linear style influenced by the Nazarenes. Koch's recasting of Claude, purified by the Nazarenes' more 'primitive' line, became the benchmark for German landscape art and attracted international followers. Among his closest collaborators in Rome was the British landscape artist George Wallis, who had settled in Italy in 1788 and who was feted in Germany for the purity of his linear and heroic style.

National Identity

The triumph of the Nazarene aesthetic accompanied the emergence of German national identity in the wake of the Napoleonic occupation. Critics like Friedrich Schlegel promoted a distinctive and patriotic Germanness in response to the occupation and a reassessment of the German contribution to Western art. Dürer and his northern Renaissance contemporaries were exalted as exemplars of something distinctively German. Wilhelm Heinrich Wackenroder, one of the critics who defended Friedrich against the criticism of Ramdohr over his Tetschen altarpiece, lamented: "At the time Albrecht Dürer was holding his brush, a German had still a special and excellent character of stability in the arena of nations in our part of the world; and his pictures bear truly and clearly, not only in their features and in the entire external appearance but also in their inner spirit, this serious, straight and strong nature of the German character. In our times, this German character as well as German art has been lost . . . . German art was a pious youth reared among kinsmen, within the walls of a small town; now he is older, he has become an ordinary man of the world, who has wiped from his soul, together with the provincial customs, his feeling and his special character."[12] Something of the impulse to recover a distinctive German spirit is found in Carl Philipp Fohr's *Ruins of Hohenbaden*, one of thirty drawings made for the Grand Duchess Wilhelmina of Hesse in a sketchbook of antiquities and sites of historical interest around Darmstadt. The Duchess's family had allied itself to Napoleon but the Emperor had recently fallen from power and the lands of the Grand Duchy of Hesse were being contested at the Congress of Vienna the very year Fohr began his project. There is an inevitable ambiguity in Fohr's drawing. Is this a castle that has rightly sunk into decline, reclaimed by nature after being eclipsed by a new political order? Or is this a mournful scene of nature overtaking a monument of German culture and civilization? This is something more than a straightforward topographical view. The German lettering on the original mount and the *faux naïf* style of draughtsmanship mark Fohr's desire to recover a German spirit thought dormant since the death of Dürer.

In Britain the young Samuel Palmer was equally concerned about rediscovering a lost tradition but his approach was strikingly different. In 1824 he had formed 'The Ancients', an artistic brotherhood seeking to revive the religiosity of art before the High Renaissance, something almost certainly inspired in part by a knowledge of the Nazarene brotherhood in Rome. In 1826 he left London for Shoreham, a village in Kent, and devoted his time to working from nature. At the end of 1828 he told his father-in-law John Linnell that "I am desperately resolved to try what can be got from drawing from nature. I think the pictures at our exhibitions seem almost as unlike nature as they are unlike fine art." But his study of nature was not mere description. A High Church Anglican, Palmer sought to represent the spiritual world beyond the world of matter, arguing that "creation sometimes pours into the spiritual eye the radiance of Heaven". Creation, for Palmer, was nothing "other than the veil of heaven, through which her divine features are dimly smiling; the setting of the table before the feast, the symphony before the tune, the prologue to the drama; a dream of antepast and proscenium of eternity."[13] Like Wackenroder, Palmer admired the northern Renaissance artists whose work he came to know through Blake and Linnell, and he mocked those antiquated cognoscenti who continued to dismiss their work as "Gothick and barbarous".[14] In his own work

Palmer rode roughshod over the materialist and rationalist aesthetics of the Enlightenment. Artists a generation earlier would have approached the trees he depicted at Lullingstone as prime examples of the Picturesque, an aesthetic category based on the idea that the roughness of nature could excite the retina and thus produce pleasure to the viewer. Palmer rejected this reductive thinking, arguing that contemplating created things such as mountains or the moon "not only thrill the optic nerve, but shed a mild, a grateful and unearthly lustre into the inmost spirits, and seem the interchanging twilight of that peaceful country, where there is no sorrow and no night". But, unlike the Germanic linearity of the Nazarenes, Palmer's drawing of the oaks in Lullingstone Park is encrusted with opaque gouache to the point of three dimensionality as he worked to capture what he called "the moss, the rifts, and barky furrows, and the mouldering grey" of the trees.[15] Palmer's choice of subject celebrates the stability of aristocratic landowning, and the densely layered technique itself functions as a visual equivalent of the organic and evolving nature of English society so celebrated by the British conservative imagination.

Romantic Sublime

In Britain and Germany artists like Palmer or Friedrich were seeking an art that would express the spiritual dimension of nature. If we want a definition of this Romantic aspiration, we can do no better than the poet Novalis's description of Friedrich's art as one which gave "profound meaning to the commonplace, an aura of the mysterious to the ordinary, the distinction of the unknown to what is perfectly familiar and to the finite a glint of the infinite".[16] It was this Romantic rejection of Enlightenment certainties that so disturbed Ramdohr when contemplating Friedrich's Tetschen altarpiece and moved Wackenroder, supporting Friedrich, to argue that feeling was more important than eighteenth-century good taste.[17] In his own defense, Friedrich asserted that "every truthful work of art must express a definite feeling, must move the spectator either to joy or to sadness, to melancholy or to light-heartedness".[18] He believed his art conveyed God's creative and beneficent hand, and these impulses have been linked to his Lutheranism, in particular to the influence of Ludwig Kosegarten's sermons, in which nature itself was considered sufficient to express the doctrine of the faith.[19] But, as Joseph Koerner has observed, the apparent emptiness of Friedrich's landscapes often left contemporaries bemused; without the conventional attributes of landscape art they struggled to interpret the scenes before them.[20] Friedrich's *Moonlit landscape* is characteristically pregnant with meaning yet eschews definitive interpretation. A wayside shrine to Our Lady of Sorrows stands beside a closed gate. A distant church nestles beneath a range of hills beneath a glowing full moon that illuminates the whole landscape. There are no figures. When pitted against the moon, the shrine and church seem no more than symbols of man's attempt to understand something infinitely greater than religion and popular piety can comprehend. Instead we can only intuit that higher truth through a created thing, the majestic moon, but it cannot itself be fully disclosed. V.A. Zhukovskii thus described Friedrich as an artist whose works contained in them "something more than what meets the eye" and whose approach to nature was to find "everywhere in it a symbol of human existence".[21] Related to this tendency is his remarkable drawing of the Jakobikirche in his native town of Greifswald imagined as a ruin, the vanishing point centered on the altar, where, instead of finding the Lutheran sacrament, two travelers gape in incomprehension, as if discovering the remains of a fallen and now bewildering civilization. It is notable Wackenroder and many of Friedrich's fellow Romantics such as Schlegel and the Nazarenes converted to Catholicism and found in the Church a sure repository of eternal truth. But Friedrich's doubtful attitude towards the institutional church anticipates that of Kierkegaard, and his liberal nationalism which aspired to German unity and political reform was set against the Nazarene reverence for established order and tradition.[22]

Friedrich's reputation declined after 1820 and his work slipped into obscurity for the rest of the century.[23] Koch's style continued to define landscape art, but was more closely allied to German natural philosophy than to Friedrich's

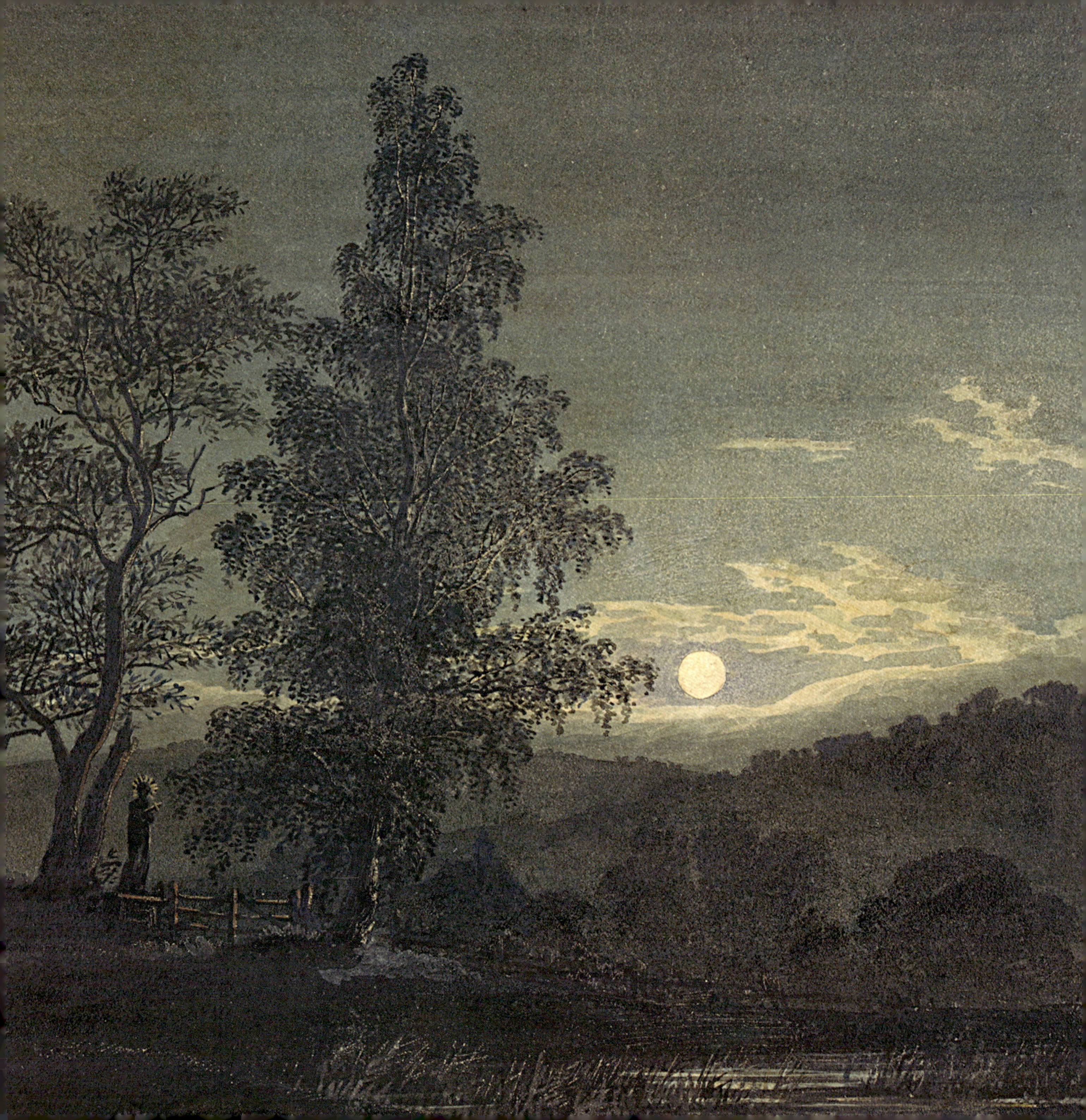

artful idealism and imaginary compositions. Koch's brief return to Austria from 1812 to 1813 to evade the French occupation of Rome only reinforced the association of his linear style with Germanic culture and resistance.[24] By 1825 King Ludwig I of Munich was cultivating Nazarene taste at his court and recruited the leading Nazarene painter Peter Cornelius to head the Munich Academy.[25] Friedrich's own disciple, Ernst Ferdinand Oehme, who left Dresden for Italy in 1822 funded by Crown Prince Friedrich August, felt compelled to adopt something of Koch's heroic manner, albeit, as Hans Neidhardt has pointed out, half-heartedly.[26] His Alpine landscape captures the sharp outlines and epic qualities of Koch's manner but nonetheless preserves something of the pregnant solitude familiar to Friedrich. It recalls the words of another of Friedrich's pupils, Carl Gustav Carus, who wrote: "Climb to the topmost mountain peak, gaze out across long chains of hills, and observe the rivers in their courses and all the magnificence that offers itself to your eye – what feeling takes hold of you? There is a silent reverence within you; you lose yourself in infinite space; silently, your whole being is purified and cleansed; your ego disappears. *You are nothing; God is all.*"[27]

By 1819, when J.M.W. Turner made his first visit to Italy, he already had a reputation as Britain's leading landscapist, even though what little was known of his work came only through reproductive prints. He must have been aware of Koch but seems not to have sought him out in Rome. He showed nothing publicly there until his return in 1828, when he stayed for the winter and mounted a small exhibition of two landscapes and an historical picture. These met with general bewilderment and even outright ridicule. Koch dismissed the "world famous" Turner's work for its indistinctness, complaining that it was "beneath all criticism and the mediocrity that is admired by the modern world", and concluded that it was "in the English milord taste of Anglican fantasy".[28] Turner's earlier view of the Alps helps clarify the gulf that divided British and German approaches to landscape. In 1802 Turner had toured the Alps on foot, filling his sketchbooks with motifs to turn into finished watercolours on his return. His *Mont Blanc from Courmayeur*, made in 1810, represents the Brenva Glacier at Val Veni with Mont Blanc looming in the distance. This region was of particular importance as one of the main crossing-points in the Alps, that great physical and psychological barrier separating northern and southern Europe. Whereas Oehme's Alps are sharply delineated from a high vantage point with an air of reverent tranquillity pervading the scene, Turner's Courmayeur is dwarfed by the vast mountain and the glacier is cloaked in vaporous obscurity. Turner's warmth of colour and sublime mist convey a sense of awesome power, suggesting the fragility of human life clinging to this remote, mountainous region. Topography here takes on profound questions – the relationship between man and nature, human life, culture, religion and civilization. It was these qualities that led Ruskin to call Turner's work in this vein "Turnerian Topography" noting that "the aim of the great inventive landscape painter must be to give the far higher and deeper truth of mental vision, rather than that of the physical facts".[29]

The technical sophistication in Turner's handling of watercolour includes washing, rubbing out, sponging and scratching the paper with a fingernail kept unusually long for the purpose and with the end of the brush. Unlike the fastidious linearity of much German draughtsmanship, such bravura effects had by the 1830s become a hallmark of British art, especially of landscape drawing. The impact of the work of John Robert Cozens and Thomas Girtin in the 1780s and 1790s had helped shift British practice away from careful outlines and smooth watercolour washes towards a consciously mannered technique in which light and shade as well as colour took precedence over form. In so far as linearity had become associated with revolutionary politics in Britain – in 1807 Ramsay Richard Reinagle stood ready to denounce Koch's friend George Wallis for his democratic principles should he ever return to Britain – this coloristic approach had an affinity with the counter-revolutionary stance of the British state.[30] Little wonder Koch contemplated Turner's work with incomprehension, while many British critics saw the 'German style' as cold and unlike nature. Yet, while artistic and political paths had diverged since Cozens and Hackert had exchanged ideas in Naples, German and British Romantic draughtsmen were nonetheless united in seeing landscape art as a genre of significant moral value; in seeking a revivified representation of the natural world; and in a commitment to landscape as an art revealing higher truths than any rote philosophy could express.

1 Friedrich's remark was reported by his friend, the Russian poet Vasily Zhukovskii: see Schönle 2000, p. 108.

2 Honour 1979, pp. 59–60.

3 For this distinction see Alpers 1983, p. 147.

4 Johann Wolfgang von Goethe to Johann Peter Eckerman, 10 April 1829, quoted in Gage 1980, p. 219.

5 Lenz 1989, p. 29.

6 Thomas Jones, *Memoirs*, p. 117.

7 While they certainly met in 1782, it is possible that the two also met on Cozens's earlier visit to Italy in 1776. See Oppé 1952, pp. 141–42; and New Haven 1980, p. 54.

8 Beckett 1962–68, vol. 6, p. 72.

9 See Christoph Heilman, 'Dillis und die Landschaftsmalerei in England und Frankreich', in Munich 1991, pp. 14–37.

10 See Leslie 1843, p. 41.

11 Vaughan 1994, p. 143.

12 Wilhelm Heinrich Wackenroder, 'Memorial to Our Worthy Ancestor Albrecht Dürer', trans. Elizabeth Gilmore Holt, in Schiff 1988, pp. 56–57.

13 Samuel Palmer to John Linnell, 21 December 1828, quoted in Lister 1974, I, p. 50.

14 There was a growing circle of enthusiasts for German Romantic thought in London who had come to know the work of Dürer and other Northern artists: see London 2005, pp. 101–02.

15 For a discussion of German linearity versus Palmer's surfaces see London 1972, p. 15.

16 As quoted in Christina Grummt, 'Introduction', in Madrid 2009, p. 9.

17 Vaughan 1994, p. 8.

18 As quoted in Vaughan 1994, p. 16.

19 Koerner 2009, p. 78.

20 Koerner 2009, p. 16.

21 Schönle 2000, p. 243.

22 Koerner 2009, p. 56.

23 Koerner 2009, p. 166.

24 Vaughan 1994, p. 38.

25 Vaughan 1994, p. 142.

26 Hans Joachim Neidhardt, 'Ernst Ferdinand Oehme and Caspar David Friedrich', in London 1972, p. 46.

27 Carl Gustav Carus, 'Letter II', in Carus 2002, p. 87.

28 Josef Anton Koch in *Moderne Kuntschronik* (1834), quoted in Gage 1969, p. 104.

29 John Ruskin, *Modern Painters Vol. IV*, in Cook and Wedderburn 1904, VI, p. 35.

30 Farington 1978–84, VIII, p. 2953.

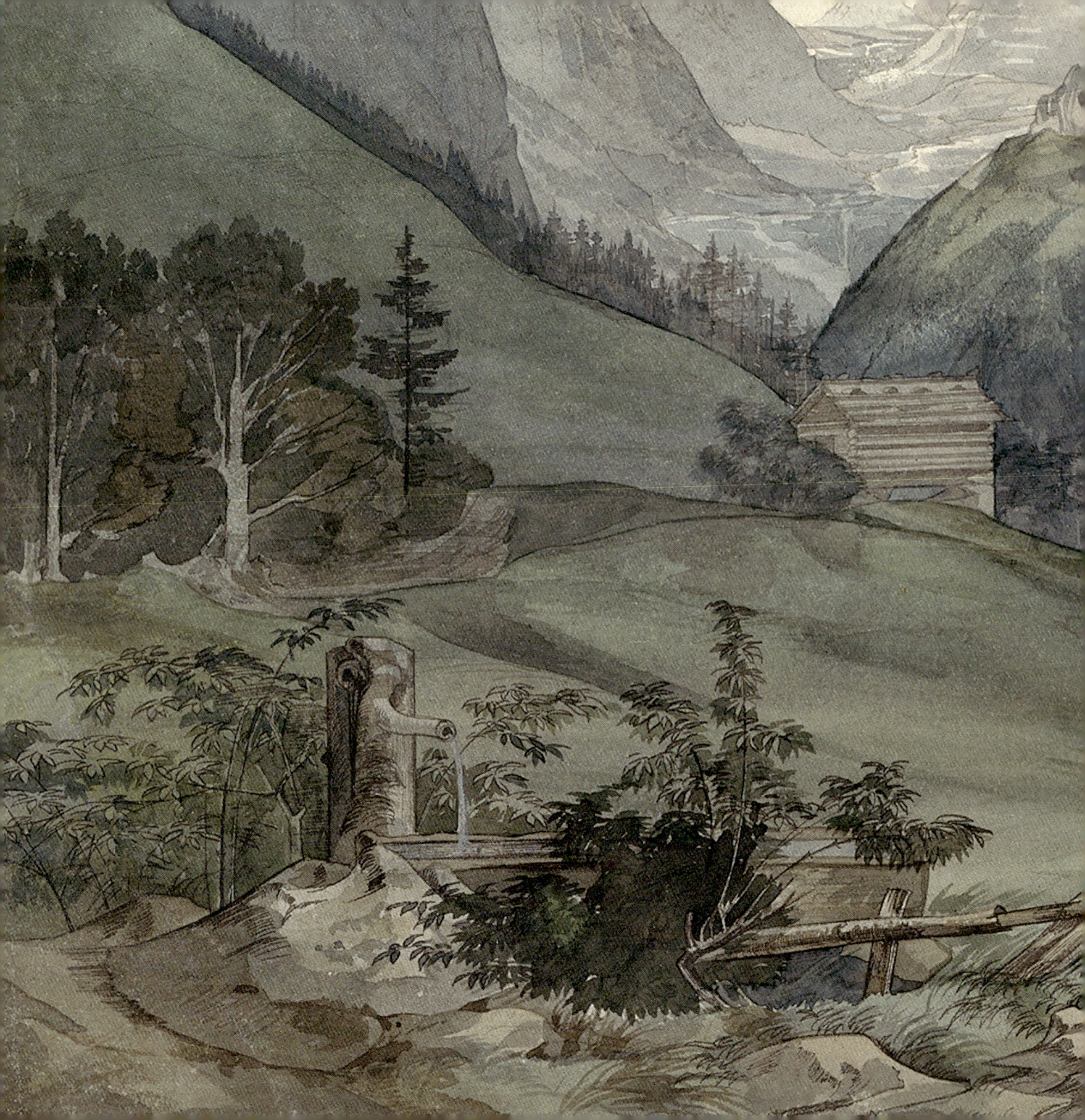

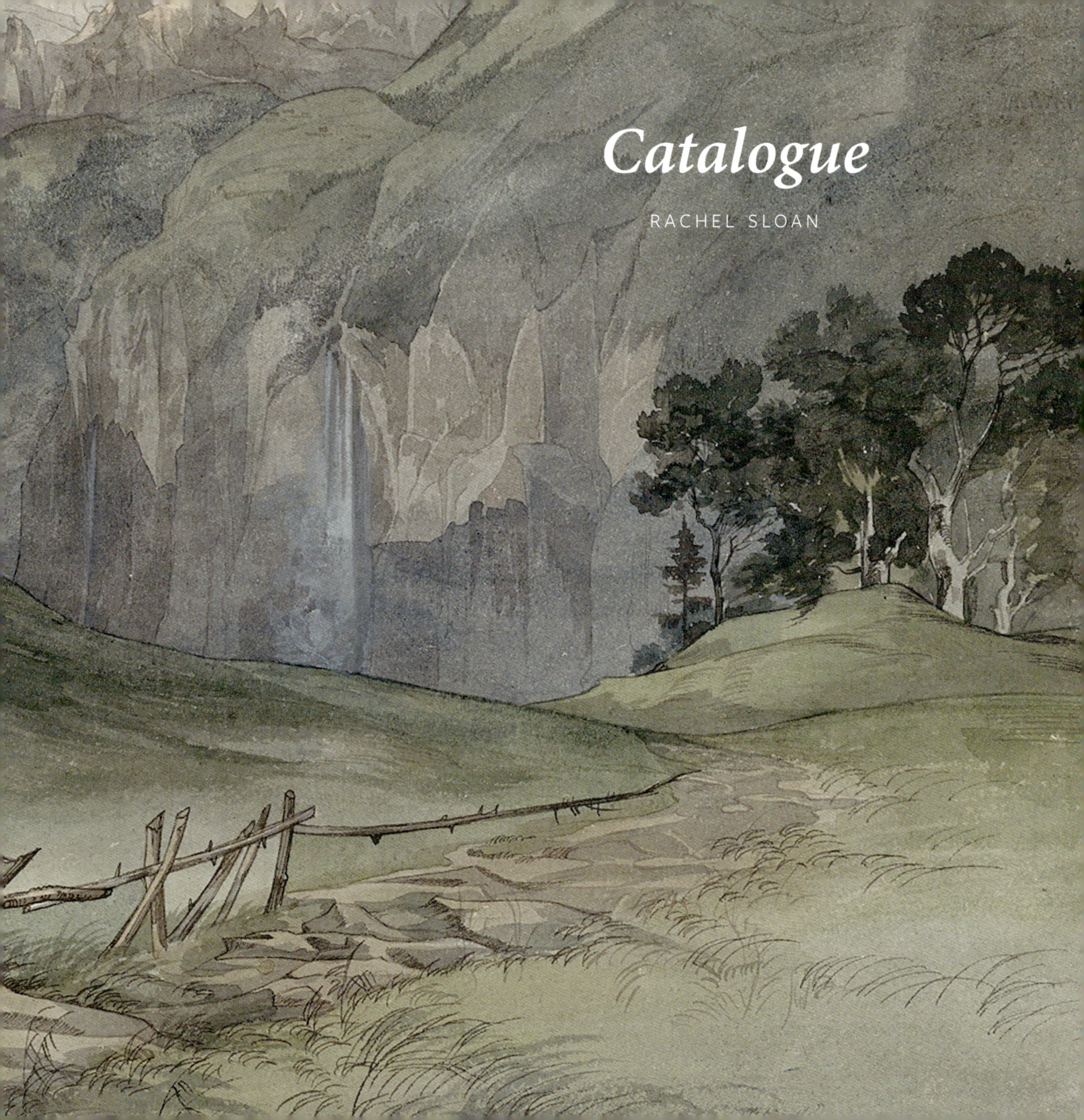
Catalogue
RACHEL SLOAN

THOMAS GAINSBOROUGH
Sudbury 1727–1788 London

Wooded upland landscape with cottage, figures and cows,
c. 1785

Although Gainsborough owed his fame during his lifetime to his oil portraits, he was also a prolific draughtsman whose landscape drawings were prized by collectors. As a young man, he had sketched directly from nature, his approach guided by the realistic landscapes of Dutch artists such as Jacob van Ruisdael (1628/29–1682), but from 1759, when he moved to Bath and established himself as a portraitist, he rejected his "schoolboy stile [sic]"[1] in favour of creating compositions inspired by his own imagination and the use of table-top models, whose elements – such as pebbles and lumps of coal for rocks and broccoli for trees – he could move and recombine to produce endless variations.

The present drawing has been situated towards the end of Gainsborough's career, a period in which he drew with exceptional freedom and in which his style synthesized the open, light-filled compositions of Claude Lorrain and the rich incidental detail of Dutch landscape, overlaid with his own distinctive aesthetic.[2] Gainsborough experimented tirelessly with media and papers; he was one of the first British artists to use wove paper, as he does here, taking advantage of its smoothness to stump the black chalk so finely as to create wash-like effects. Indeed, this drawing showcases his ability to create a varied range of tones and textures with a single medium, from the soft, limpid greys of the distant hills to the startling intensity of the dynamic strokes describing the foreground trees and figures.

Gainsborough firmly believed in the potential of landscape to serve as a vehicle for emotion, appealing to the imagination and the heart as much as – or more than – the intellect. Rustic fantasies such as this, in a similar manner to those of Johann Georg Wagner (cat. 2), are representative of the type of landscape drawing most prized in the later eighteenth century and from which Romanticism sprang – and which it ultimately questioned.

Black chalk with stumping on wove paper,
282 × 367 mm
The Courtauld Gallery, Samuel Courtauld
Trust, D.2007.DS.16

WATERMARK

J WHATMAN

PROVENANCE

Given by the artist to Dr William Pearce
(c. 1751–1842); by whom presented to his
solicitor, Henry Whitehead; by descent to Miss
Frances Whitehead; her sale, Sotheby's, 30
November 1978, lot 139; John Morton Morris
& Co.; Dorothy Scharf (1942–2004); Scharf
Bequest, 2007

NOTES

1 Hayes 2001, p. 30.
2 Both John Hayes and Hugh Belsey date the
drawing to the mid 1780s, a period in which
Gainsborough produced some of his most
intense black-chalk drawings: see Hayes
1983, no. 955, p. 387, and Belsey 2008,
no. 955, p. 455.

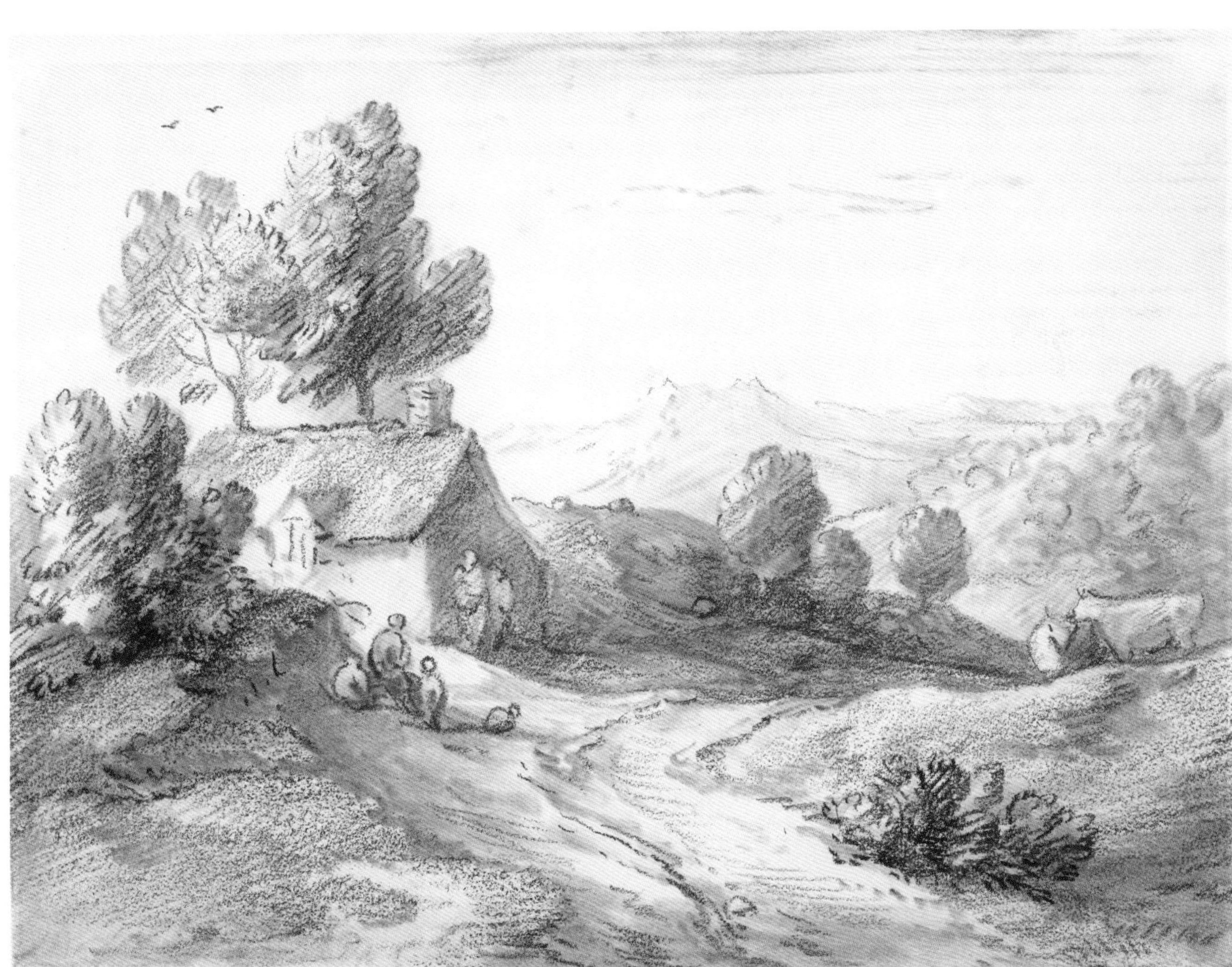

Wooded landscape with stream and oxcart on road, 1760s

Wagner, the son of two artists (Johann Jakob and Maria Dorothea Wagner), was trained by his parents and by his uncle, the Dresden landscapist Christian Wilhelm Ernst Dietrich (1712–1774). Most of his brief career, cut short by his death at the age of twenty-two, was spent in Dresden, where he taught at the academy from 1765. The present drawing is a representative example of his small surviving oeuvre.

Wagner specialized in landscape and bucolic genre scenes. Here the gently rolling hills in the distance and the soft, even light establish a peaceful, pastoral mood and suggest that Wagner's aim was the creation of an ideal landscape, probably not done directly from life. Like Jakob Philipp Hackert's drawings (cat. 4), this work unites elements of the classicizing Claudean tradition with the attention to everyday detail of the Dutch artists who worked in Italy, most notably in the treatment of the ox cart at right, but on a more intimate scale. The stylized, almost calligraphic treatment of the foliage of the foreground trees supports the supposition that the drawing was created entirely from the imagination, as Gainsborough (cat. 1) also preferred to do; however, the subtle handling of grey and brown wash to render the variegated texture of the bark suggests that some prior study from life may have informed the composition.

A number of Wagner's paintings and drawings were reproduced in the form of etchings by contemporary artists in Germany and France, including Hackert. These etchings were admired and collected in Britain long after his death, as were his drawings; indeed, the present drawing entered a British collection in the nineteenth century.

Pen and brown ink, black chalk and grey and brown wash on laid paper, 194 × 277 mm
The Courtauld Gallery, Samuel Courtauld Trust, D.1952.RW.65

INSCRIPTIONS

Recto, lower left: collector's mark of Henry Stephen Olivier (L.1373). Verso: inscribed in graphite, upper left, *Wagner*; lower centre, *MJ* (?); in a different hand, lower right, *12* (twice); upper right, *4/4*

PROVENANCE

Henry Stephen Olivier (1796–1866); by descent to Maud Olivier; Christie's, 21 July 1948 (?as part of lots 10, 11 or 14); Sir Robert Witt; Witt Bequest, 1952

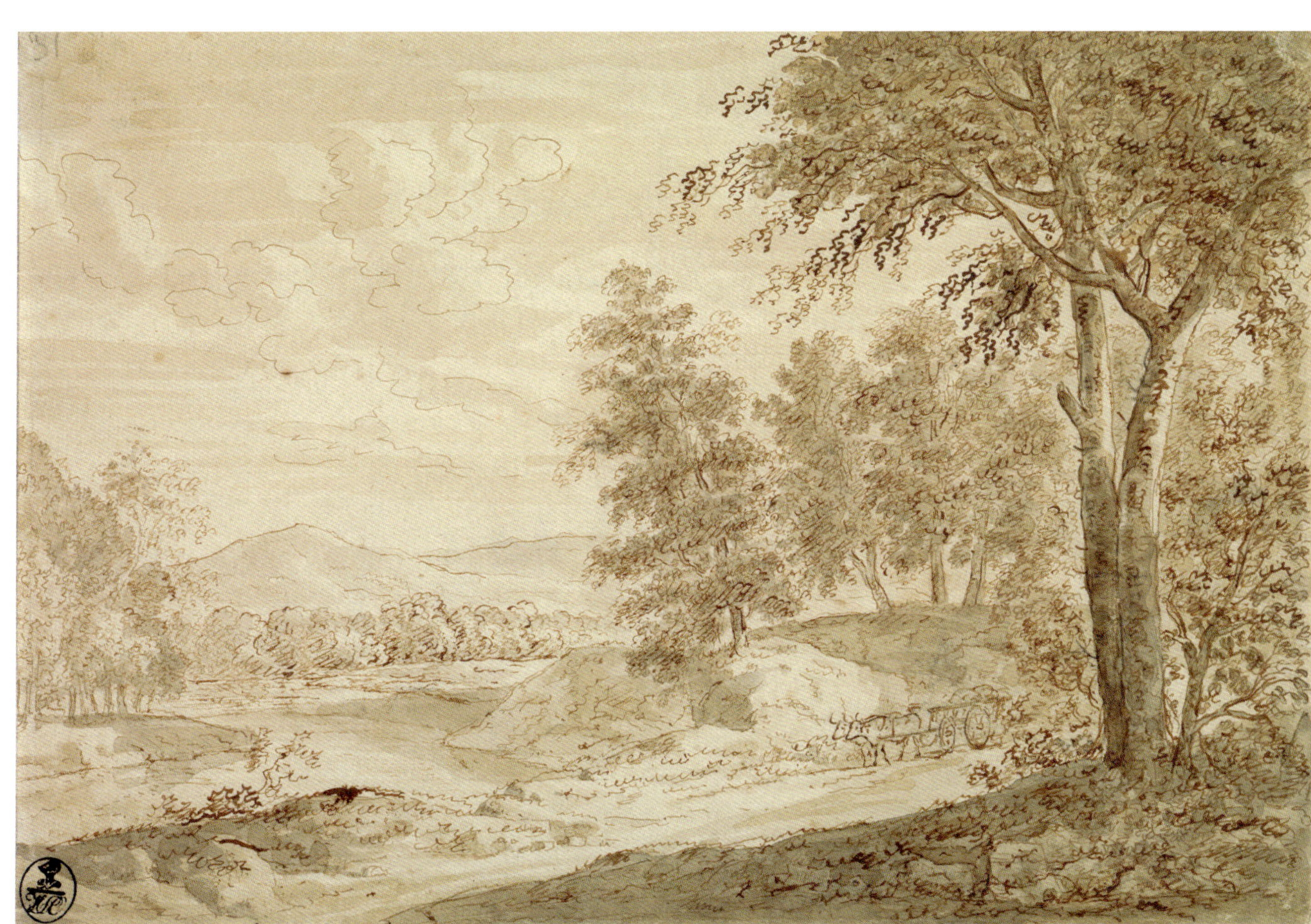

Old Windsor Green, 1762

Sandby, who began his career as a topographical draughtsman for a
military survey of the Highlands, is traditionally regarded as 'the father
of English watercolour'; while this is not strictly true in chronological
terms, he was the first artist to derive his reputation primarily from
work in this medium.[1] From 1748, when his brother, Thomas, was
appointed Ranger of Windsor Great Park, he was a frequent visitor to
Windsor, which furnished material for numerous watercolours, many of
which were made with public exhibition in mind.

Sandby's watercolours are what were known as 'tinted' or 'stained
drawings', the outlines laid in with graphite and pen and filled with
transparent washes which allowed the white of the paper to shine
through. The expansive size and format of the present work, which
consists of two sheets of different sizes joined together, suggests that
he set out expressly to make a large-scale watercolour and would have
worked mostly in the studio, perhaps after making sketches out of
doors; both this practice and the panoramic format were informed by
his early survey work. Although large areas of the reserve are left bare
and the staffage only hinted at, the inscriptions in Sandby's hand, which
he ostensibly added in preparation for the sale of his studio contents,
attest to the fact that by the early nineteenth century such views were
prized items for collectors' portfolios, even unfinished. A related
aquatint exists, with the watercolour's composition compressed into a
more conventional format.[2] Such manipulation of the site's topography
refutes the notion that Sandby was a mere recorder of fact, for which
Gainsborough criticized him, and suggests that his closely observed
scenes were less removed from the more idealized views of Jakob
Philipp Hackert (cat. 4), Gainsborough (cat. 1) and Wagner
(cat. 2) than might initially be assumed.[3]

Pen and grey ink and watercolour over
graphite on two sheets of laid paper, joined,
350 × 792 mm
The Courtauld Gallery, Samuel Courtauld
Trust, D.1967.WS.86

INSCRIPTIONS

Recto: inscribed in graphite, lower left: *Old
Windsor Green*, and signed and dated in pen
and iron gall ink, lower right *At Old Windsor,
P.S. 1762*; inscribed by the artist in pen and
carbon-black ink wash above inn sign *Good
Entertainment For man and horse*; numbered
in a later hand in graphite, top, right of centre,
212. Verso: visible through backing, fragmentary
sketch of a tree at left-hand edge in pencil, with
further inscriptions

WATERMARK

I/IHIS/I VILLEDARY and a fleur-de-lys within a
shield surmounted by a crown

PROVENANCE

Mrs J.B. Young; Mr and Mrs William Wycliffe
Spooner; Spooner Bequest, 1967

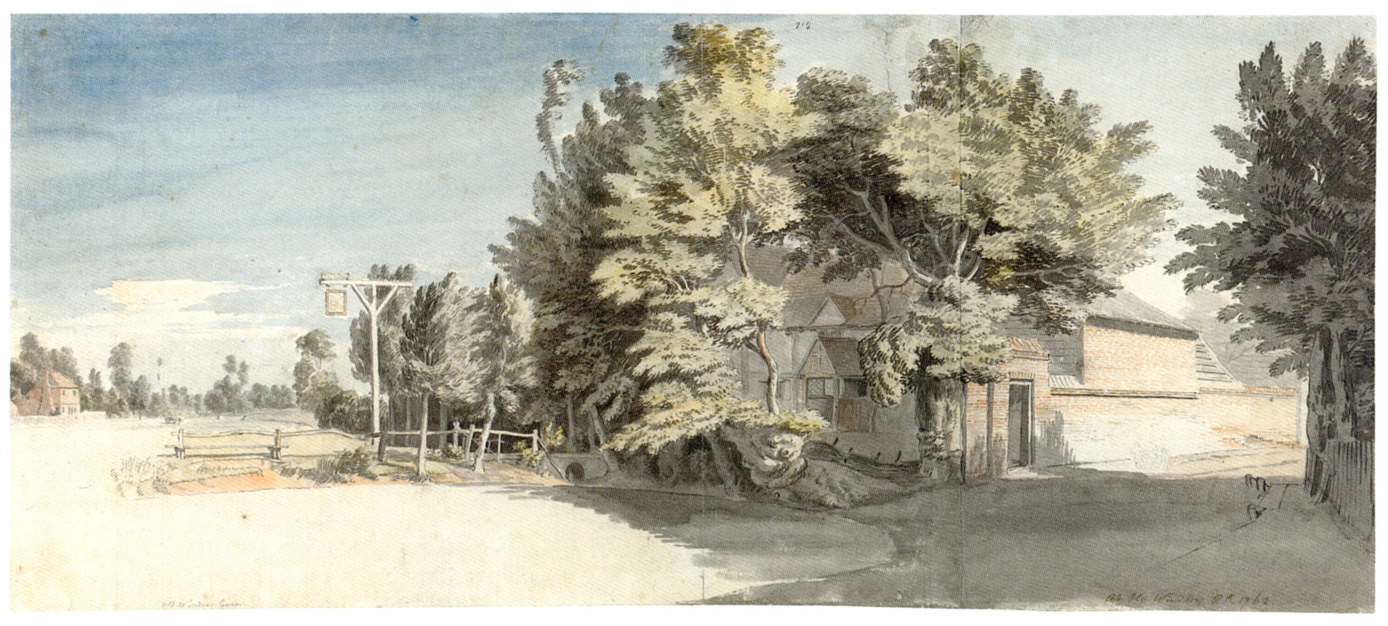

NOTES

1 For an overview of the early history of
   watercolour in Britain, including earlier
   practitioners such as Francis Place
   (1647–1728), see Hardie 1966.

2 *The Fox Public House on Old Windsor Green*,
   n.d., Royal Collection (Windsor), 814335.
   The watercolour is unlikely to have been
   conceived as directly preparatory for the
   print, which Ann Gunn tentatively dates to
   between 1778–1789 (email correspondence,
   18 October 2013); indeed, the crease down
   the middle of the work suggests that Sandby
   simply kept it as studio material. I am
   grateful to Jane Roberts for discussing both
   works at length with me.

3 In a letter to a patron in 1764, Gainsborough
   declined a request to paint 'real views from
   Nature in this country', recommending
   Sandby instead as 'the only Man of Genius…
   who has employ'd his Pencil that Way'
   (Hayes 2001, p. 30) As Matthew Hargraves
   notes, the compliment conceals criticism,
   given that Gainsborough considered
   ideal landscapes derived from the artist's
   imagination to be of a higher order
   (New Haven 2007, p. 17).

JAKOB PHILIPP HACKERT
Prenzlau 1737–1807 San Piero di Careggio

4

View of the Villa of Maecenas and the Falls at Tivoli, 1783

The son of the portraitist Philipp Hackert (d. 1768), Jakob Philipp Hackert trained at the academy in Berlin and travelled widely, settling permanently in Italy in 1770. He worked primarily in the environs of Rome and Naples, both of which boasted significant communities of artists from northern Europe, many of whom, like Hackert, emulated the luminous ideal classical landscapes of Claude Lorrain. Goethe, a great admirer of Hackert, wrote his biography and stressed his then-unorthodox practice of sketching out of doors.

Tivoli, near Rome, was a favourite subject, and Hackert devoted several drawings and paintings to its landmarks, including the great cascade and the Roman ruins then known as the Villa of Maecenas.[1] This large, highly worked pen-and-wash drawing, probably intended for a collector, would not have been made on the spot: an open-air study in pen and ink, now in the Berlin Kupferstichkabinett (432–1990), allowed him to record the structure of the composition. Despite the title, the ruined villa, pushed into the upper left corner, does not dominate the composition. The true subject, rendered with great subtlety, seems to be water and its reflections, from the waterfalls and their spray to the river flowing past in the foreground, creating a sense of evanescence and impermanence. The juxtaposition of the generalized background, which, rendered with soft stippling, appears to fade away, and the wealth of closely observed detail in the foreground, including the hard-edged outlining of foliage and the contemporary costume of the figures at lower right, undercuts the harmonious mood of Claudean idealism and reveals Hackert's debt to a parallel, more descriptive northern European tradition, particularly the landscapes of Jacob van Ruisdael and of the Dutch artists active in Rome in the seventeenth century.

Hackert's work was collected by several British amateurs, including Richard Payne Knight (1750–1824), one of John Robert Cozens's most important patrons.[2] Cozens's own monumental approach to landscape may have been informed by his knowledge of Hackert's work; indeed, the two artists met in Naples in 1782.

Pen and brown ink, brown ink wash over graphite on laid paper, 536 × 746 mm
The Morgan Library & Museum, purchased as the gift of Mrs Douglas Auchincloss, 1972.17

WATERMARK

On primary support, indecipherable due to secondary support

INSCRIPTION

Upper left corner: *Les Ruines de la Villa de Mecenes à Tivoli, Ph. Hackert, f. 1783*

PROVENANCE

Peter Rowlands, London

NOTES

1   A painting of the same subject, also made in 1783 (St Petersburg, Hermitage, GE 7156) shares a very similar composition with the present drawing; given the differences in composition and its high degree of finish, the drawing is probably not a study for the painting but an independent, albeit related, work of art.
3   On Hackert's reception in Britain, see Simon Reynolds, 'Jakob Philipp Hackert und die britischen Sammler', in Weimar and Hamburg 2008, pp. 70–74.

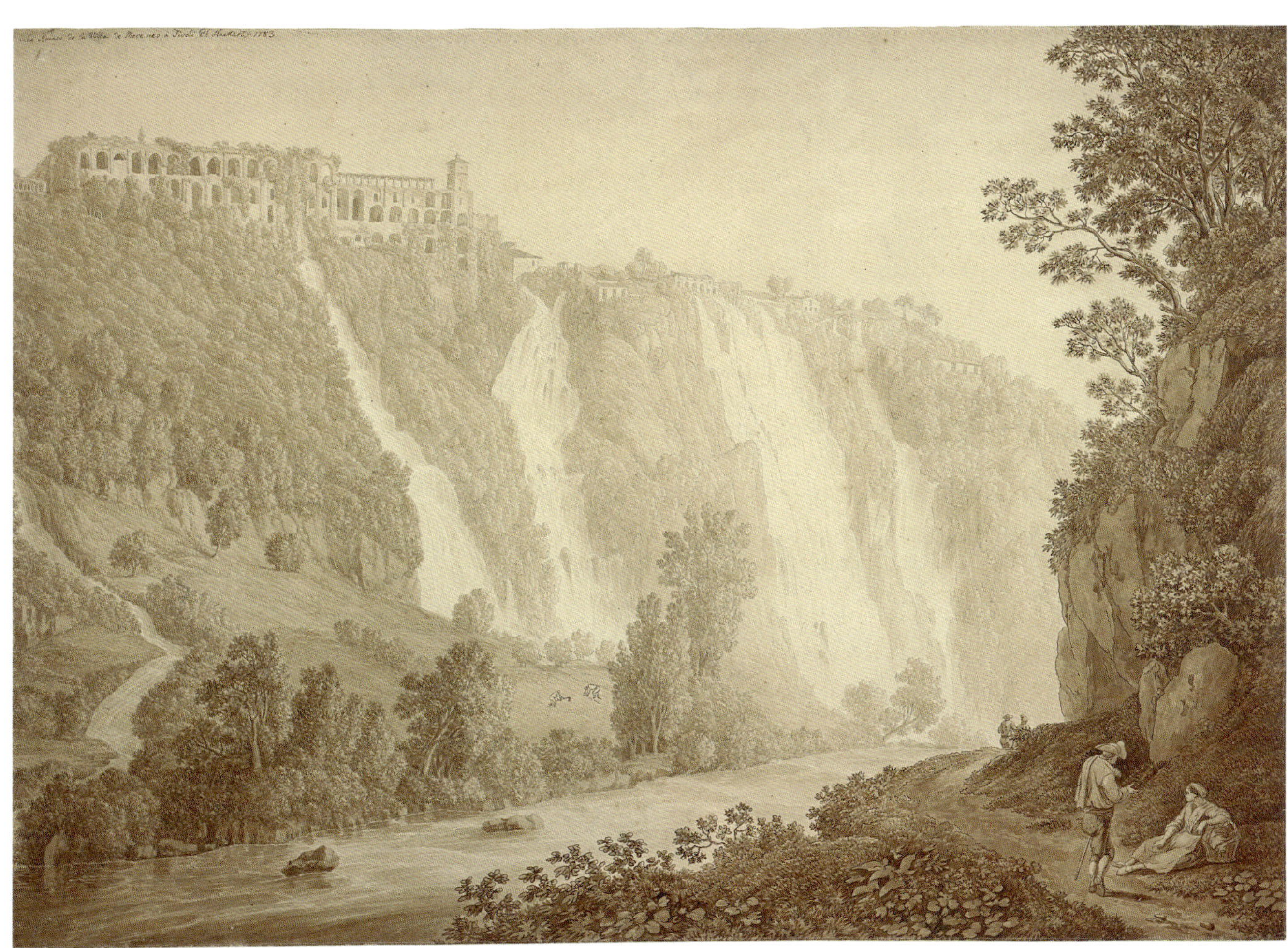
Ruines de la Villa de Mecenas à Tivoli Ph. Hackert f. 1783.

Russia *c.* 1717–1786 London

5

A blasted tree in a landscape, c. 1780

Little is known of Alexander Cozens's early life. Born in Russia but educated in England, he travelled widely as a young man, meeting the French landscape and marine painter Claude-Joseph Vernet (1714–1789), who encouraged him to sketch from nature, in Italy. By 1746 he had arrived in London, where he earned his living as a drawing master.

Cozens's pedagogical background led him to publish *An Essay to Facilitate the Invention of Landskips* (1759), in which he propounded a system for creating landscape drawings based on 'blots' – near-abstract brush drawings intended to suggest the shapes of different types of landscapes. A finished drawing could be created by laying a sheet of paper, made transparent with a turpentine-based varnish, over a blot and tracing, and then elaborating the forms in brush and wash, working from light to dark. Cozens expanded upon his system in several further treatises; the composition of the present drawing suggests that it was based on plate 7 in *The Various Species of Composition of Landscape in Nature*, 'A large object, or a cluster of large objects, or more than one of either, near the eye'. In this case, the 'large object' is a blasted tree, a symbol of divine wrath and a favourite motif of Romantic artists in both Britain and Germany. The drawing of the outlines, which appears to have been done entirely with the point of the brush, has been added on top of the washes. Cozens considered this technique closer to the experience of viewing nature itself than the method of setting lines down first and filling them in, used by Sandby and others (cat. 3).[1] Far from producing a formulaic oeuvre, Cozens's systems provided a structure within which the imagination could flourish. Rather than being tied to the forms of a real landscape, he could use the 'blot' as a springboard; although it might incorporate elements observed in nature, the drawing was almost purely imaginary and, more often than not, an expression of the awe and fear evoked by the sublime.

Cozens's work excited the admiration of younger artists, including Joseph Wright of Derby (1734–1797) and John Constable, and was a decisive influence on his son, John Robert Cozens (cat. 14).

Point of the brush, brown ink and wash with traces of graphite on laid paper, 315 × 405 mm
The Courtauld Gallery, Samuel Courtauld Trust, D.1967.WS.29

INSCRIPTIONS

Recto: signed in pen and grey ink on the mount, lower left corner, *Alexr. Cozens*; inscribed with letter *B* in pencil in upper right corner; blind stamped lower left corner with the letter *W* (collector's mark of Benjamin West, L.419). Verso: inscribed *A 21365* in graphite in a modern hand

WATERMARKS

Primary support: D&C / B enclosed within a shield; secondary support: D&CBLAUW / IV

PROVENANCE

Benjamin West, PRA; J.M. Reveley; Mr and Mrs William Wycliffe Spooner; Spooner Bequest, 1967

NOTE

1 Cozens wrote that "in nature, forms are not distinguished by lines, but by shade and colour": Cozens 1786.

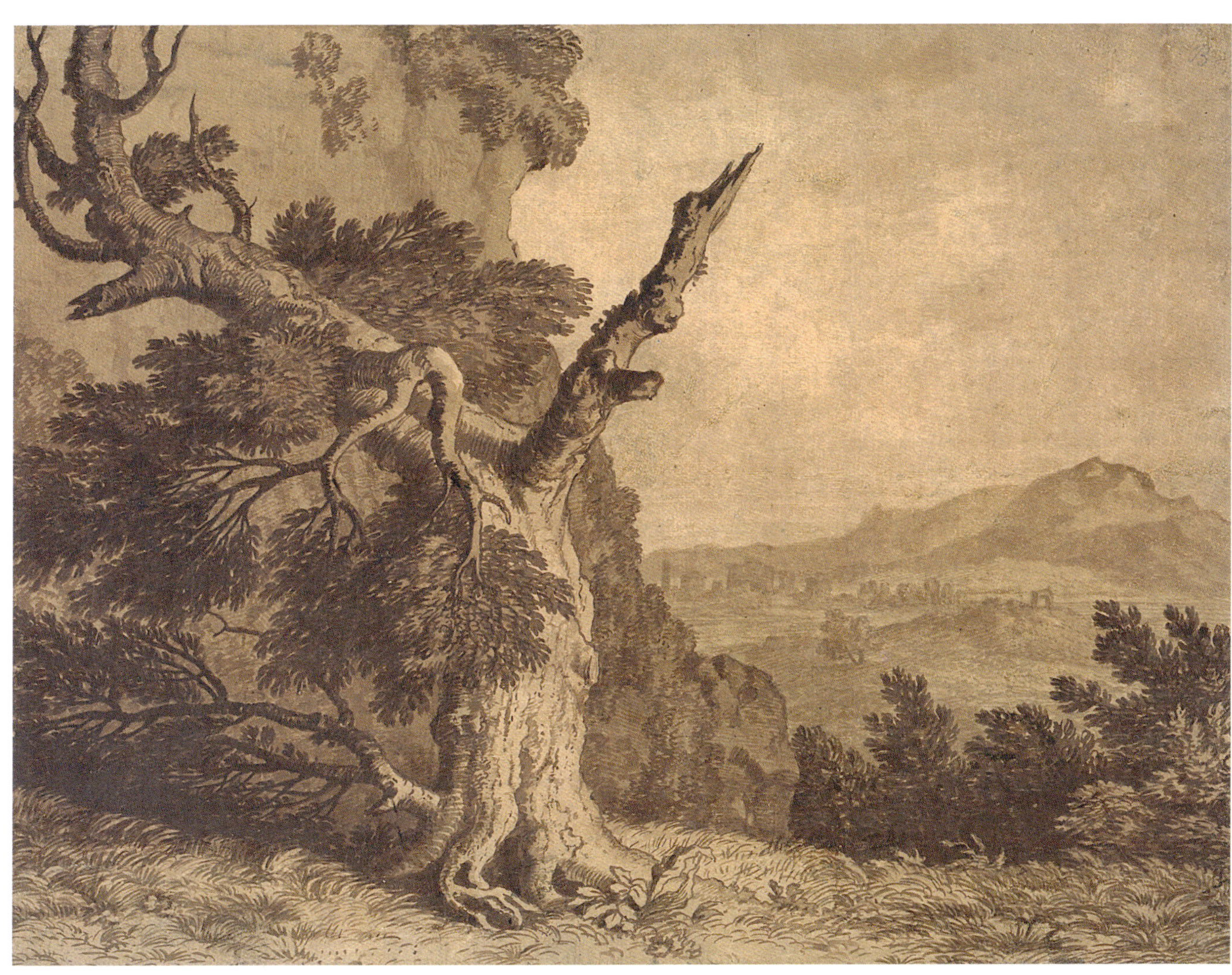

6

JOHANN GEORG VON DILLIS
Grüngiebing 1759–1841 Munich

Beech trees in the English Garden, Munich, after 1811

A pioneer of the *plein-air* oil sketch in Germany, Dillis first began to make such studies during a sojourn in Rome in 1794–95. At around the same time he acquired the patronage of Benjamin Thompson, Count Rumford (1753–1814), an American-born British scientist closely involved with the Bavarian government. Rumford and the 2nd Viscount Palmerston, with whom Dillis travelled extensively, seem to have introduced him, via prints, to the work of contemporary English artists including John Robert Cozens and Thomas Jones.

Dillis is known to have sketched in the Englischer Garten – Munich's new public park, modelled upon English landscape gardens, in whose creation Rumford was instrumental – from the time of its opening in the 1790s. An inscription on the verso of the present work, which names the location as 'near the Aumeister' (an inn in the park built in 1810–11) suggests that it was painted around or after 1811. The greater part of the composition is likely to have been painted on the spot, although Christoph Heilmann has suggested that Dillis added the smaller tree at left (the only one depicted at eye level) in the studio.[1] The distinct, flickering brushstrokes, particularly noticeable in the foliage, suggest a rapid execution, with Dillis working quickly to capture the pale blue sky and golden light of an early morning and the impression of leaves being shaken by a breeze. The tiny figure striding between the two larger trees gives a sense of scale to the scene; Dillis used the same motif in a contemporary (and apparently pendant) work of identical dimensions (Winterthur, Stiftung Oskar Reinhart).

Oil over graphite on paper, mounted to cardboard, 254 × 190 mm
Thaw Collection, jointly owned by the Metropolitan Museum of Art and the Morgan Library & Museum, Gift of Eugene V. Thaw, 2009, 2009.400.48

INSCRIPTIONS

Verso: *Buchen im engl. Garten nahe beim Aumeister*

PROVENANCE

Galerie Zinckgraf, Munich; Dr. Eugen Roth, Munich (by 1961; d. 1976); by descent to private collection (1976–at least 1991); Daxer & Marschall, Munich, in 2000; Eugene V. and Clare E. Thaw, New York, by 2002–09

NOTE

1   Munich 1991, no. 23, pp. 104–05.

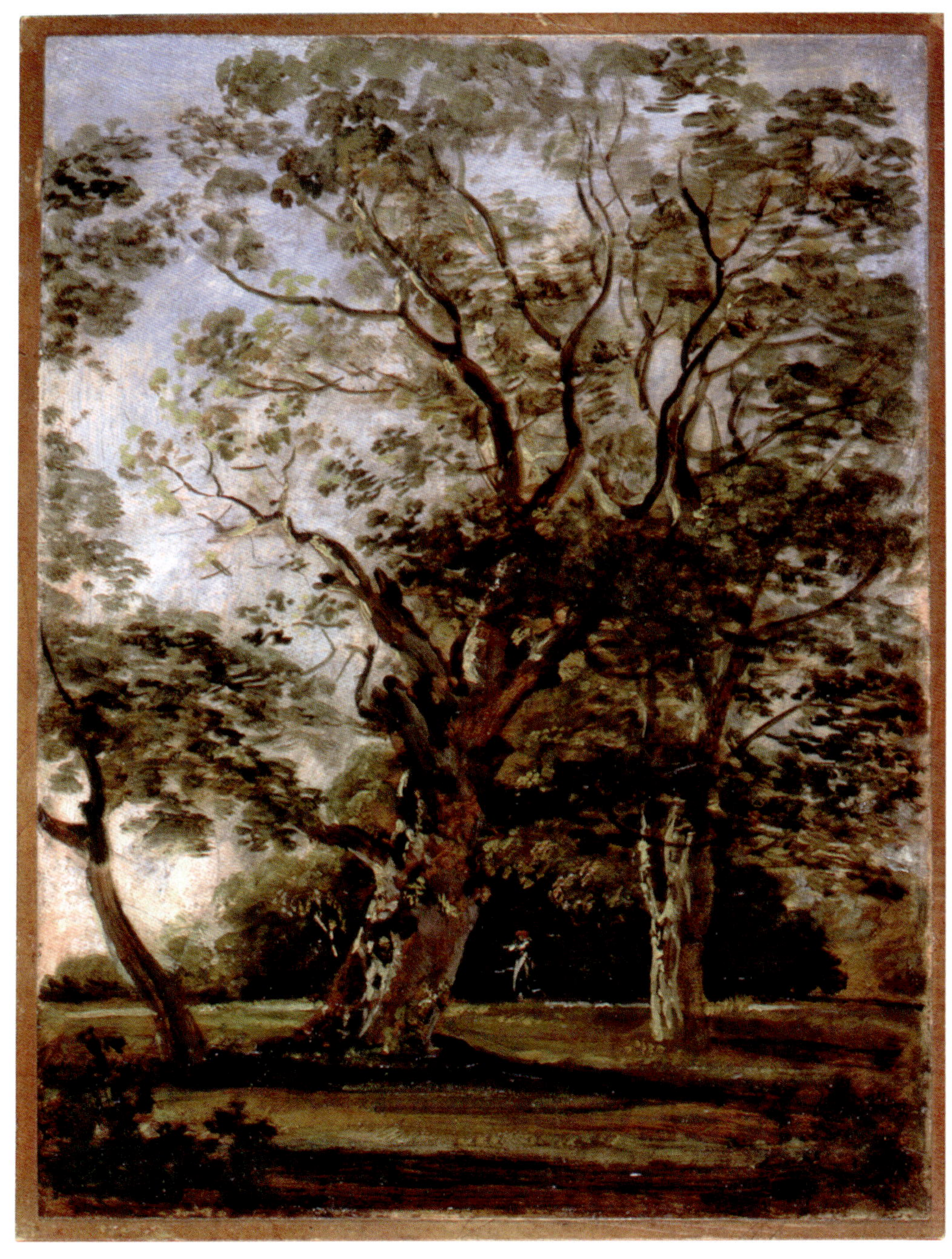

JOHANN GEORG VON DILLIS

Grüngiebing 1759–1841 Munich

7

Cloud study, *c.* 1810–1820

Although cloud studies had first emerged as a distinct genre in
the seventeenth century, they became a characteristic element of
Romantic landscape drawing, most famously so in the work of Dillis,
Johan Christian Dahl (cat. 8), and John Constable (cat. 9). Bolstered
by current theoretical writings on clouds by Luke Howard (*On the
Modification of Clouds*, 1803) and Goethe (*Schriften zu Meteorologie*,
1815), these artists seized on cloud studies as a means of studying
nature directly without recourse to academic formulae. Capturing such
ephemeral, ever-changing forms also presented an appealing challenge.

Dillis produced some 150 cloud studies, most of which, like the
present work, were made in white chalk on sheets of blue laid paper
(the torn edges at the bottom of this study are typical and suggest that
his studies were done on the same stock of paper). He signed and dated
few of them, and, as the entire body of studies formed part of his estate,
clearly considered them private exercises rather than saleable works.
Most Romantic cloud studies took the form of oil sketches; Dillis was
relatively unusual in using a coarse blue paper to create the ground,
exploiting its textural possibilities in the interaction of the rough
surface and the diaphanous touches of chalk to suggest the evanescent
wisps of the clouds. Crucially, the coloured paper – here beautifully
preserved – represented a solution to the oil sketcher's problem of
needing to record both the colour of the sky and the colours and forms
of the clouds scudding across it. Dillis was able to use the paper itself
to represent the sky, thus allowing him to devote his attention fully to
recording the movement of the clouds.[1]

White chalk on blue laid paper, 251 × 387 mm
The Morgan Library & Museum, Thaw
Collection, 2010.132

WATERMARK

CS in rectangle

PROVENANCE

Estate of the artist; purchased from the artist's
descendants by the Historischer Verein von
Oberbayern (Upper Bavarian Historical
Association) in 1897; Karl & Faber, Munich,
May 1978; C.G. Boerner, Düsseldorf, 1978;
private collection, Germany, 1978; C.G. Boerner,
New York; Eugene V. and Clare E. Thaw,
New York

Exhibited in London only

NOTES

1 Dillis is known to have used a range of
shades of blue paper to represent different
types of light and atmospheric condition:
see Barbara Hardtwig, 'Johann Georg von
Dillis and the European cloud study', in
Hamburg 2002, p. 15). It should be stressed
that while Dillis was somewhat atypical
among his contemporaries in using blue
paper for his cloud studies, such a technique
had precedents in the seventeenth century:
see John Gage, 'Clouds over Europe,' in
Edinburgh 2000, pp. 128–30.

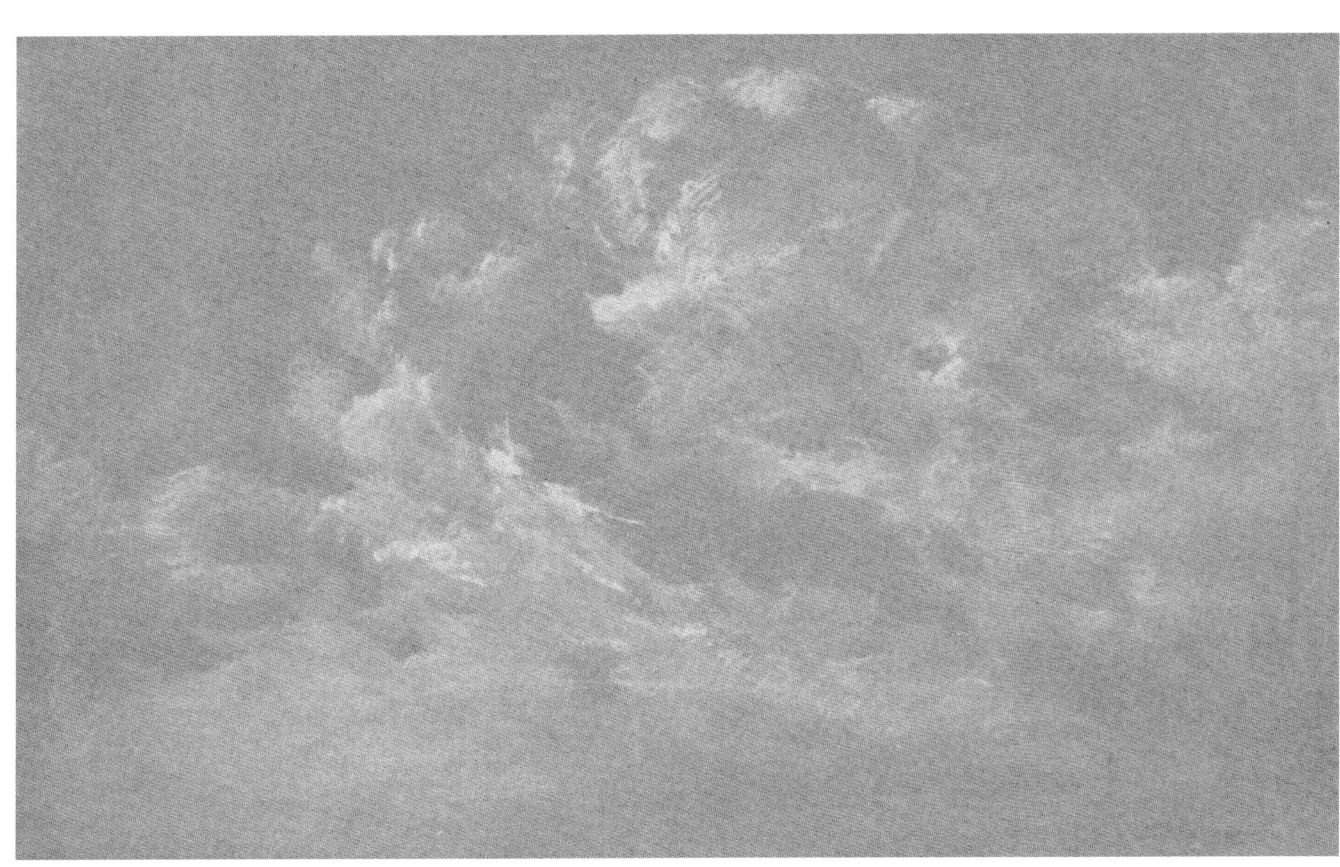

8

JOHAN CHRISTIAN CLAUSEN DAHL
Bergen 1788–1857 Dresden

Cloud study, 1828

Born in Norway, Dahl spent the greater part of his career in Germany, based primarily in Dresden, where he befriended Friedrich. Dahl and Friedrich were regarded during their lifetimes as complementary artists, Friedrich the idealist and Dahl the naturalist, although the distinction between the two was not as sharp as this view implies.

Dahl produced more than 300 *plein-air* oil studies over the course of his career, a practice that, like Dillis, he first adopted during a tour of Italy. One of the oil sketch's most skilful practitioners, he boasted that he could paint three sketches of the same cannon volley. Although no doubt an exaggeration, such speed was vital for cloud studies, which sought to capture both changing light and constantly shifting and disintegrating forms. Like Constable, Dahl often dated his cloud studies to the day; an inscription on the verso of this sketch indicates the time of day depicted as evening, an assertion supported by the pale overall tone of the sky and the pink light of the setting sun that streaks the clouds near the horizon. Although he painted quickly, Dahl's touch is light and sensitive, in keeping with the sketch's small scale; the paint surface is smooth, with few individually distinguishable brushstrokes. The cluster of poplars at lower centre, delineated with a few swift licks of green paint, seem to have been added primarily to anchor the composition. Although the trees effectively transform the work from a pure cloud study into a landscape, Dahl's main concern appears to have been with capturing the atmospheric effects of the sky.

Oil on paper, mounted on cardboard,
121 × 162 mm
Thaw Collection, jointly owned by the Metropolitan Museum of Art and the Morgan Library & Museum, Gift of Eugene V. Thaw, 2009, 2009.400.33

INSCRIPTIONS

Recto: dated and initialled (upper left): *d. 9 May 1828. D.* Verso: in black ink by Thorleif Wasteson, *Bevidner herved at denne studie/ h11,5 + b14,7 cm er malt av J.C.C. Dahl/ Oslo 5/9 45 Th. Wasteson*, over earlier inscription in graphite containing the number 10557; in dark brown ink, *No 164./ Johann Chr. Cl. Dahl/ Naturstudie, Abendhimmel/ ueber Berghorizonth mit Pappeln/ gemalt d. May 1828./ 16'b. 11 ½' h.*; in brown ink by the artist's son Johann Siegwald Dahl, *d. 17 Nov. 85/ mit Mastix f. [?]/ gefirnisst*; and in light brown ink by the artist's daughter-in-law Catharine Dahl, *zur Erinnerung von/ dem Vater meines Mannes/ d.17.10.1902 Catharine Dahl*

PROVENANCE

The artist's studio; the artist's son, Johann Siegwald Dahl (1827–1902), Dresden; private collection; sale, Oslo, Blomqvist, 13 November 2006, lot 31; Eugene V. and Clare E. Thaw, New York

Exhibited in New York only

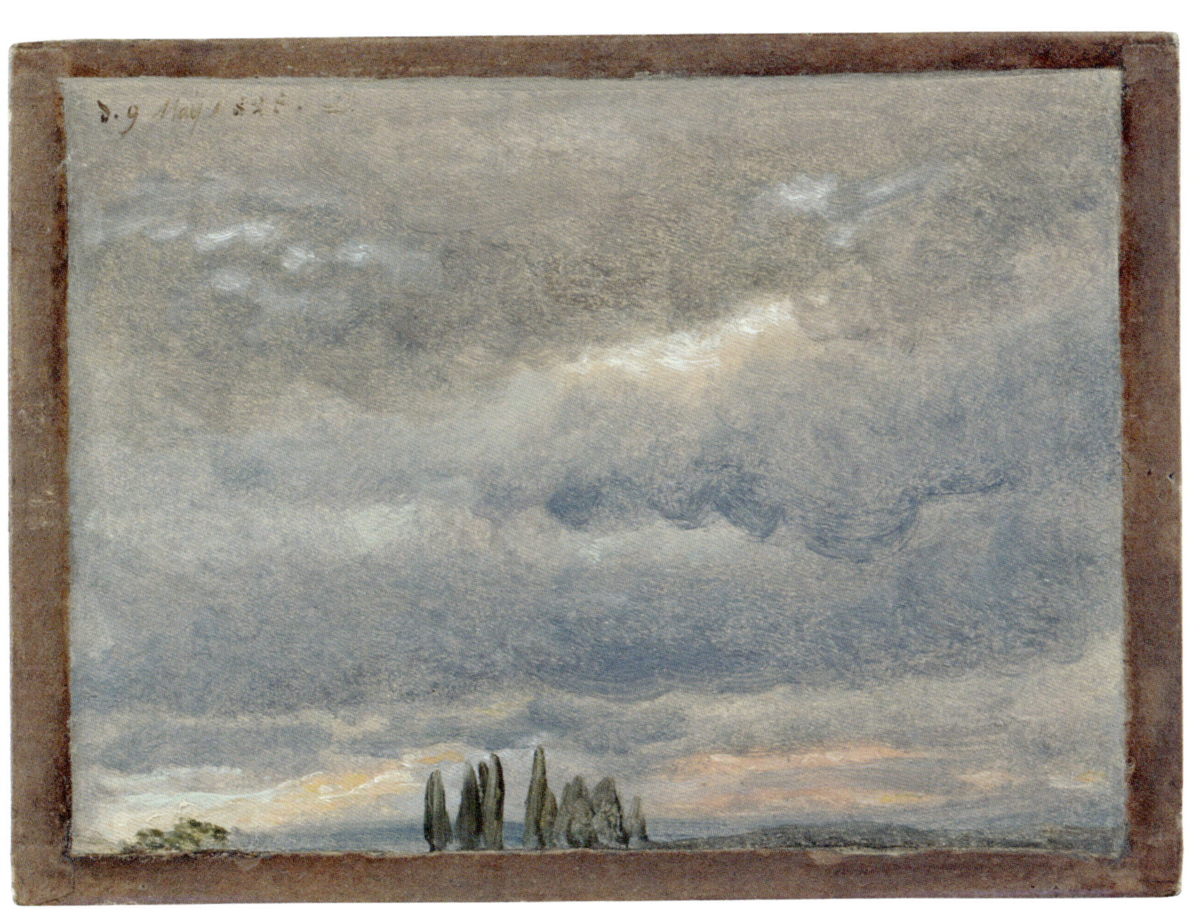
d. 9 May 1826

East Bergholt 1776–1837 Hampstead

9

Cloud study, 1822

Constable first began to study clouds in oil sketches around 1810; they remained a preoccupation over the following two decades, with his first pure cloud studies made in chalk on blue paper in 1819.[1] During the summers and autumns of 1820–23 he rented a house for his family near Hampstead Heath and there undertook several sustained campaigns of cloud studies, usually noting the date, time and weather conditions on the verso. This study, one of two he undertook the same day within less than two hours of each other, shows three banks of cumulus clouds being blown across the sky from left to right by the east wind, as indicated by the inscription.[2] Although he evidently worked quickly, aided by the use of thin, fluid paint, he was unable to capture every detail as the clouds passed, as the blue band of cloud in the middle ground, blocked in but not fully finished, indicates.

Constable's meticulous recording of the circumstances of his studies does not, however, imply a purely empirical interest in clouds, even though his curiosity about them was surely fuelled by the burgeoning contemporary interest in meteorology typified by Luke Howard's *Essay on the Modification of Clouds* (1803). In a letter to his closest friend, John Fisher, the previous year, he declared, "Skies must and always shall with me make an effectual part of the composition. It will be difficult to name a class of Landscape in which the sky is not the *'key note'*, the *standard of 'Scale'* and the chief *'Organ of Sentiment'* . . . . The sky is the source of light in nature – and governs every thing."[3] In Constable's conception of nature, a scientific interest in physical particularities and a belief that the landscape was a vehicle for emotion and a manifestation of the divine were not diametrically opposed, but inextricably linked.

Oil on two superimposed sheets of wove paper laid down on a third sheet, 305 × 490 mm
The Courtauld Gallery, Samuel Courtauld Trust, P.1952.RW.69

INSCRIPTIONS

Verso: inscribed by the artist in pen and ink, *Sepr. 21 1822. looking South/ brisk wind at East Warm & fresh. / 3 oclo afternoon*; numbered by a different hand in pencil, *5*

PROVENANCE

Paterson Gallery, 1928; Sir Farquhar Buzzard, 1937; Sir Robert Witt; Witt Bequest, 1952, with life interest to Miss Thyra Creke-Clark (d. 1974)

NOTES

1 Reynolds 1984, 1911–9.16 (private collection) and 1911.17 (Glyn Vivian Art Gallery, Swansea). I am grateful to Anne Lyles for drawing my attention to these early studies.
2 Edinburgh 2000, no. 57, p. 86.
3 Letter of 23 October 1821, Beckett 1962–68, VI, p. 77.

10

FRANCIS TOWNE

Isleworth, Middlesex 1739/40–1816 Exeter

Near Devil's Bridge, Wales, 1810

Towne, like Alexander Cozens, supported himself primarily as a drawing master and worked almost exclusively as a watercolourist. Along with John Robert Cozens, he was one of the first British watercolourists to travel extensively on the Continent, making a tour of Italy and Switzerland in 1780–81. He may have met Hackert in Rome, and almost certainly knew his work and reputation; both artists were notable for their insistence on working out of doors, Towne frequently noting on his own drawings that they were "drawn on the spot".[1]

From 1809, all of Towne's surviving work was made in sketchbooks. The present watercolour, which comes from a sketchbook in which he recorded a tour of Wales in the summer of 1810, depicts a rugged, thickly forested valley east of Aberystwyth crossed by the so-called 'Devil's Bridge' (visible, although obscured by trees, at lower centre). Wales, mountainous and remote, the grandeur and menace of its scenery evocative of the sublime, occupied a place in the Romantic imagination not dissimilar to that of Rügen for Caspar David Friedrich and his contemporaries (cat. 17), and it inspired some of Towne's most powerful work. The strongly graphic quality of the line, a distinguishing characteristic of Towne's work that recalls the earlier watercolours of Sandby (cat. 3), set him apart from his peers, particularly in a period when the painterly approach of Turner, Girtin and their contemporaries was beginning to blur the distinction between watercolour and oil painting. Towne would almost certainly have drawn the contours of the landscape on the spot, laying them in first in graphite and working them up in pen and ink, adding the watercolour washes later, in the studio.[2] Working in his typically limited palette of blues, greens and greys, here enlivened by a splash of orange in the foreground, he created a vivid sense of contrast between sunlight and cloud shadow. The panoramic format afforded by working across two sheets of the sketchbook, in tandem with the tiny stature of the single staffage figure left of centre, creates a sense of man's insignificance in the face of the vastness of nature.

Graphite, pen and grey ink, watercolour, brush and black and brown ink and opaque watercolour (dilute orange) on two sheets of off-white wove paper, 171 × 512 mm
The Courtauld Gallery, Samuel Courtauld Trust, D.1967.WS.93

INSCRIPTIONS

Verso: inscribed by the artist in graphite, *Near Devil's Bridge* and each sheet numbered *1 & 2*; towards the centre of the left-hand sheet *Join* in graphite, repeated upside down on the right-hand sheet

WATERMARKS

[WH]ATMAN / 1808 on right-hand sheet

PROVENANCE

John Herman Merivale (1779–1844); Mr and Mrs Sutton, by descent; Fine Art Society, 1961; Mr and Mrs William Wycliffe Spooner, 1964; Spooner Bequest, 1967

NOTES

1 On Towne's familiarity with Hackert, see London 1997, pp. 19–22.
2 Timothy Wilcox, email correspondence, 23 September 2013. The colour of the wash in the clump of trees at lower centre is somewhat discontinuous across the join, raising the possibility that Towne may have begun colouring one sheet alone and changed his mind after they were joined.

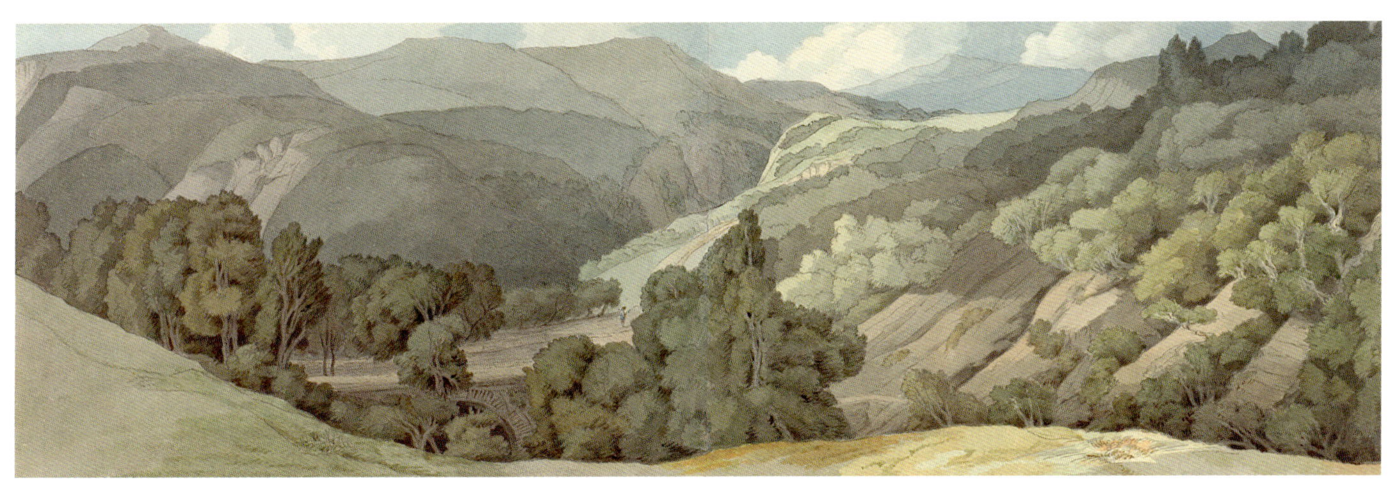

11

FRANZ KOBELL

Mannheim 1749–1822 Munich

Landscape near Munich with storm clouds, *c.* 1800

Following a sojourn in Italy sponsored by the Elector Carl Theodore – where Goethe acclaimed him as the greatest landscape painter of his time – Kobell returned to his adopted hometown of Munich and devoted himself almost exclusively to drawing. In Italy he and his brother, Ferdinand (1740–1799), had specialized in ideal landscapes influenced by the Italian tradition that nonetheless relied upon direct study from nature.

After returning to Germany, Kobell renewed his commitment to sketching from nature. The present drawing is one of a number of studies of the scenery along the River Isar near Munich in brush and wash that he produced during the first decade of the nineteenth century.[1] Although the use of ink washes probably owes something to the example of Claude Lorrain, whose landscape drawings were often executed in this medium, Kobell's primary interest appears to have been less in recording the flat, almost nondescript river landscape – although the composition is carefully structured with emphatic lines demarcating the horizon and the riverbank – and more in capturing the transitory effects of weather. The ink and wash are laid on vigorously, with flickering strokes in the foliage suggesting leaves shaken by a breeze, and the faint circle of the sun, at upper left, quickly brushed over as if to suggest clouds rolling across it. Several areas in the clouds exhibit noticeable dried droplets of ink, a testament to how swiftly Kobell worked to seize a particular moment.

The work of both Kobell brothers was known in the circle of artists gathered around Dr Thomas Monro, including Thomas Girtin, in the form of landscape etchings that would probably have been copied. The broadly applied washes in Girtin's *Near Kelso* (cat. 18) suggest, if not a familiarity with this strand of Kobell's work, then a similar concern with privileging ephemeral atmospheric effect over fine detail.

Brush and brown ink and brown ink wash over traces of black chalk and watercolour on laid paper, 176 × 218 mm
The Morgan Library & Museum, Bequest of Charles Ryskamp, 2010.55

PROVENANCE

Unknown collector, initials AOCN; Arturo Cuellar, Zurich; Charles Ryskamp; Bequest of Charles Ryskamp, 2010

NOTES

1   Others include one in the collection of the Morgan Library & Museum (2010.54) another in the Thaw Collection and seven in the Harvard Art Museums (1985.55–60 and 1985.72).

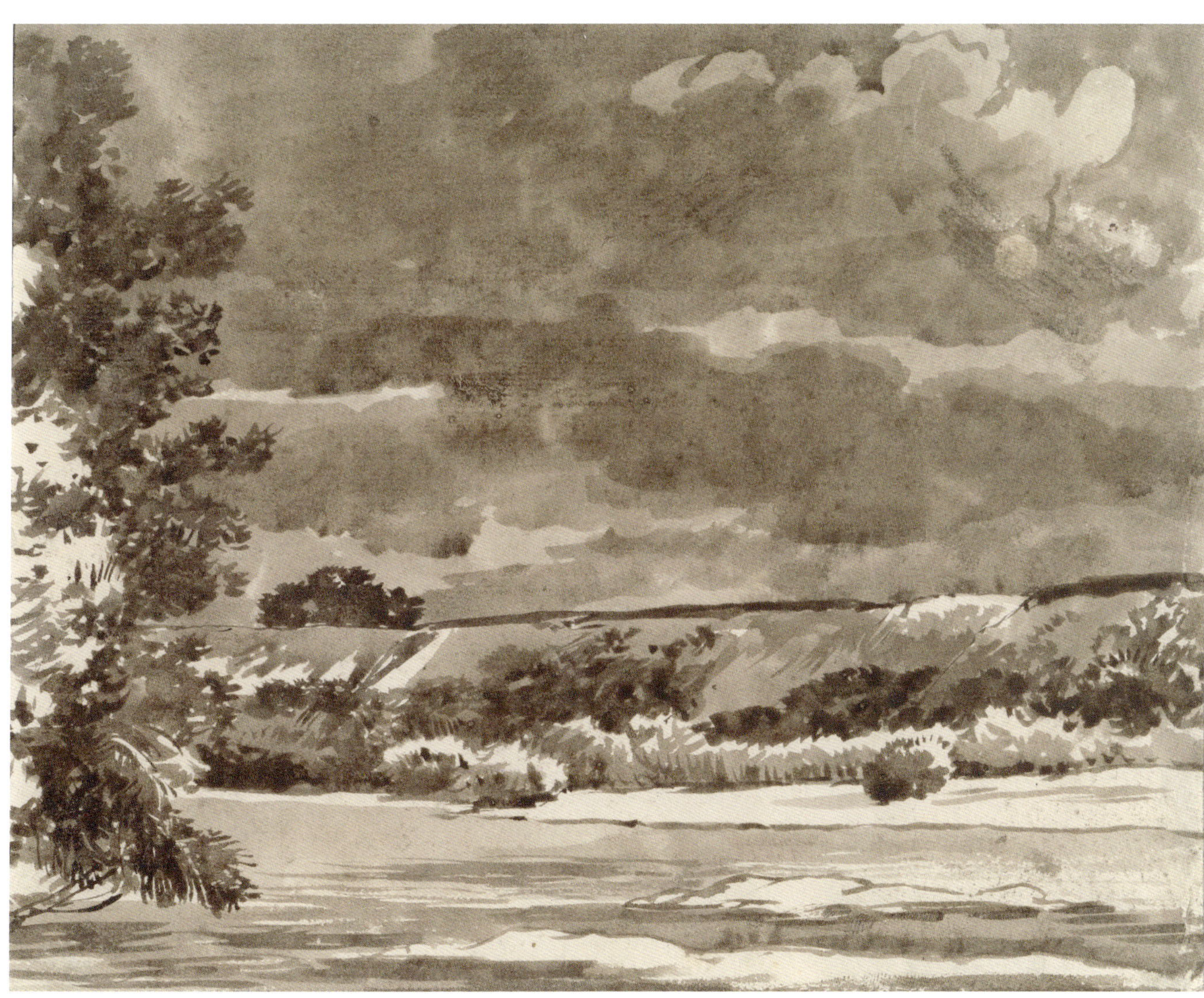

12

CASPAR DAVID FRIEDRICH

Greifswald 1774–1840 Dresden

The Jakobikirche in Greifswald as a ruin, c. 1817

The ruin is an important motif throughout Friedrich's oeuvre. This drawing, however, is unusual in transforming a building that is intact in reality – the Gothic Jakobikirche in his hometown of Greifswald – into a ruin.[1] Friedrich's reasons for doing so are complex and may encompass a critique of the current state of the Lutheran Church, an interest in the national antiquarian movement that had arisen in Germany in the early nineteenth century, and, more generally, an expression of the Christian ideas about transience, mortality and resurrection that pervade his work.

The precise dating of the drawing has been a subject of debate. Friedrich is known to have made a watercolour of the same subject in 1817,[2] as well as an oil painting (now lost) exhibited in Dresden in 1829. A perspective system centred on the altar, with the vanishing point indicated by an X and the presence of compass needle holes on all sides of the sheet indicating the orthogonals and transversals, as well as noticeable pentimenti in the heads of the figures and the column bases in the right foreground, suggest that the present drawing is preparatory for one of these works, rather than a record of a finished work. The linear, precise and dry quality of the draughtsmanship and the graphite used for shading, which evokes both shadow and the rough texture of stone, both come across as artificial rather than naturalistic.

Friedrich's interest in Gothic ruins seems to have originated at least partly in a growing national interest in historical sites that had been inspired by an earlier, parallel national antiquarian movement in Britain.[3] A number of his drawings of ruins share noticeable similarities with illustrations in British antiquarian guidebooks, although the inclusion of staffage figures in medieval costume departs from the British model and lends a certain poignancy to the scene, particularly given the male figure's gaze upward towards the crucifix. The critic E.H. Toelken said of the figures in the painting when it was exhibited in 1829 that they appeared "to contemplate the former grandeur of the building, but they are strangers from distant lands and a different time".[4]

Pen and black ink, graphite, and brown wash on wove paper; compass needle holes on all sides of sheet, 260 × 195 mm
The Morgan Library & Museum, Thaw Collection, 1996.149

INSCRIPTIONS

inscribed on verso at lower left in graphite, *5*; at upper left, [illegible] *4*

PROVENANCE

August Grahl, Dresden (1791–1886; L.1199) (?); Prof. Paul Arndt, Munich; his sale, Leipzig, C.G. Boerner, 16 May 1934, lot 74; private collection, Wittingshausen; sale, Munich, Karl & Faber, 28 November 1979, lot 35; Eugene V. and Clare E. Thaw, New York

NOTES

1   The present drawing and the two related works are not the only instance of Friedrich 'ruining' the Jakobikirche; he had also done so in a lost painting, *The Monastery Graveyard* (Börsch-Supan and Jähnig 1973, no. 254).
2   Grummt 2011, no. 763.
3   On Friedrich and national antiquarianism in Germany, see Reusch 1999, pp. 95–114.
4   Quoted in Börsch-Supan and Jähnig 1973, p. 115.

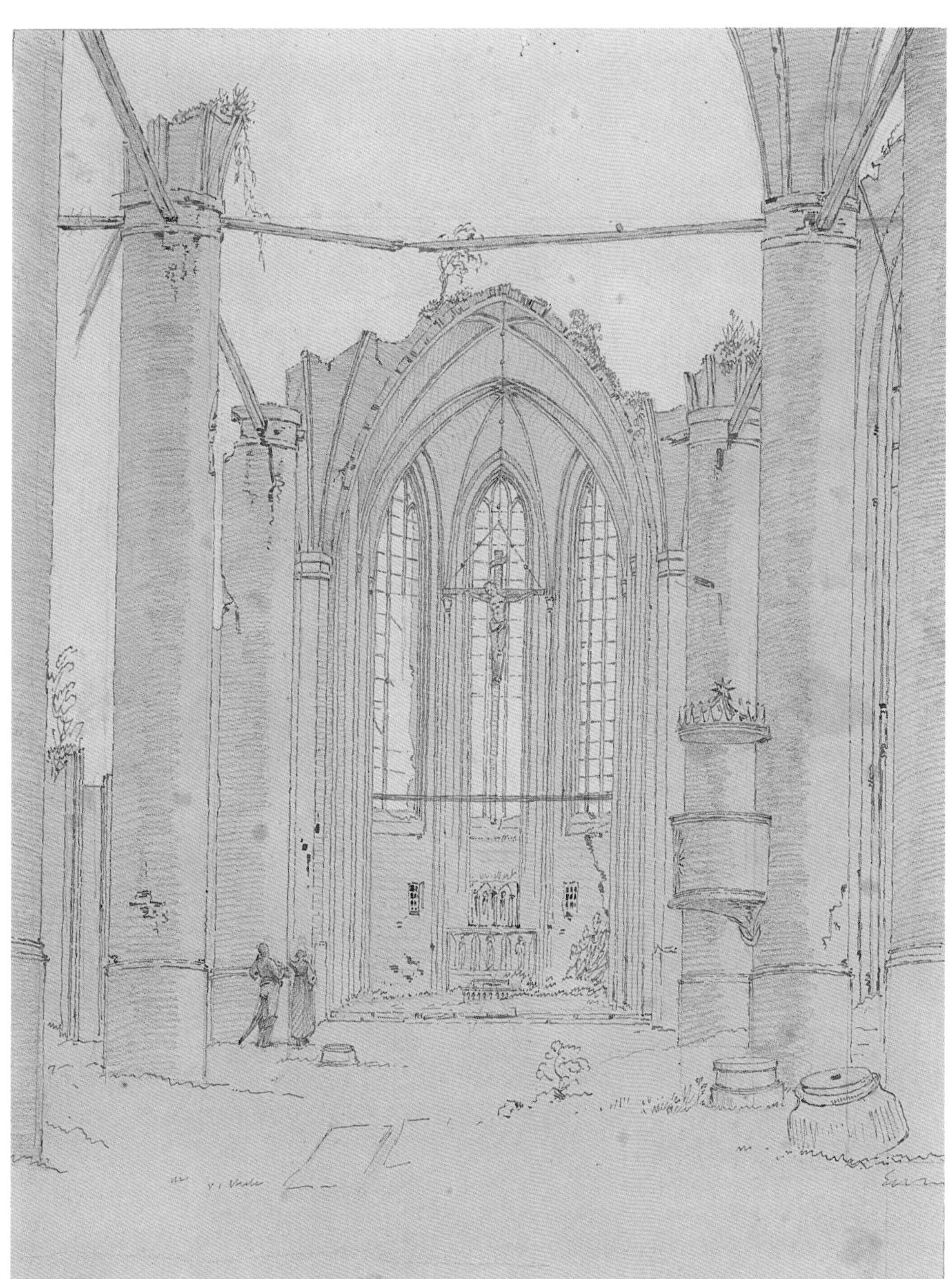

13

CARL PHILIPP FOHR

Heidelberg 1795–1818 Rome

The Ruins of Hohenbaden, 1814/1815?

Fohr, who displayed precocious artistic gifts, was taught by Friedrich Rottmann (1768–1816), the father of fellow Heidelberg artist Carl Rottmann. From 1813 until the end of his life, even after departing for Rome in 1815 to join the circle of the Nazarenes, he received regular commissions from Grand Duchess Wilhelmina of Hesse for watercolour views of landscapes in south-west Germany. These highly finished watercolours were presented to her in the form of two so-called sketchbooks, one devoted to the Neckar River valley (1813–14) and the other to the former state of Baden (1814–15).

The present watercolour comes from the now-dismembered Baden 'sketchbook'. The artist's own inscription identifies the subject as the ruined castle of Hohenbaden, built in the early twelfth century as the residence of the Margraves of Baden and abandoned in the late fifteenth century. Fohr has captured the crumbling tower and wall with characteristically sharp detail, rendering the individual stones, foliage and the bark of the tree looming in the left foreground with minute, precise brushstrokes. The deliberately naïve treatment of detail harkens back to early German art. Upon closer examination, however, it becomes clear that Fohr took considerable imaginative licence with what appears to be a straightforward transcription of a specific site. He chose to depict the ruin from an angle that diminishes its relative size at the expense of the lush vegetation overtaking it, as if to suggest the triumph of time and nature over human endeavour, a persistent Romantic theme. The composition is characterized by a stark division of light and shade, the sunlit sky and clouds – rendered in very pale (possibly faded) blue wash – casting the lower half in shadow and giving the brightly illuminated upper portion of the tower an air of fragility. All of these elements render Fohr's aim ambiguous: it is difficult to determine whether the image, produced in a period that saw Germany grappling with questions of national identity and struggling to throw off Napoleonic domination, celebrates or mourns the passing of an old order.

Watercolour on wove paper; ruled border in brown ink; partially laid down on the original green wove paper album folio, 195 × 221 mm
The Morgan Library & Museum, Thaw Collection

INSCRIPTIONS

Inscribed by the artist in pen and black ink at lower center of original green paper mount, *Die Trümmer eines Stammes der Zähringer ehemalige Wohnung*; numbered at upper right corner of original mount, *5*; printed label on verso of original green paper mount

PROVENANCE

Grand Duchess Wilhelmina of Hesse; by descent to her grandson Prince Henry of Hesse; Princess Emily of Hesse; her sale, Munich, Ludwigsgalerie, 1927; sale, Munich, Hartnung & Hartnung, 13 November 1998, lot 4047; Eugene V. and Clare E. Thaw, New York

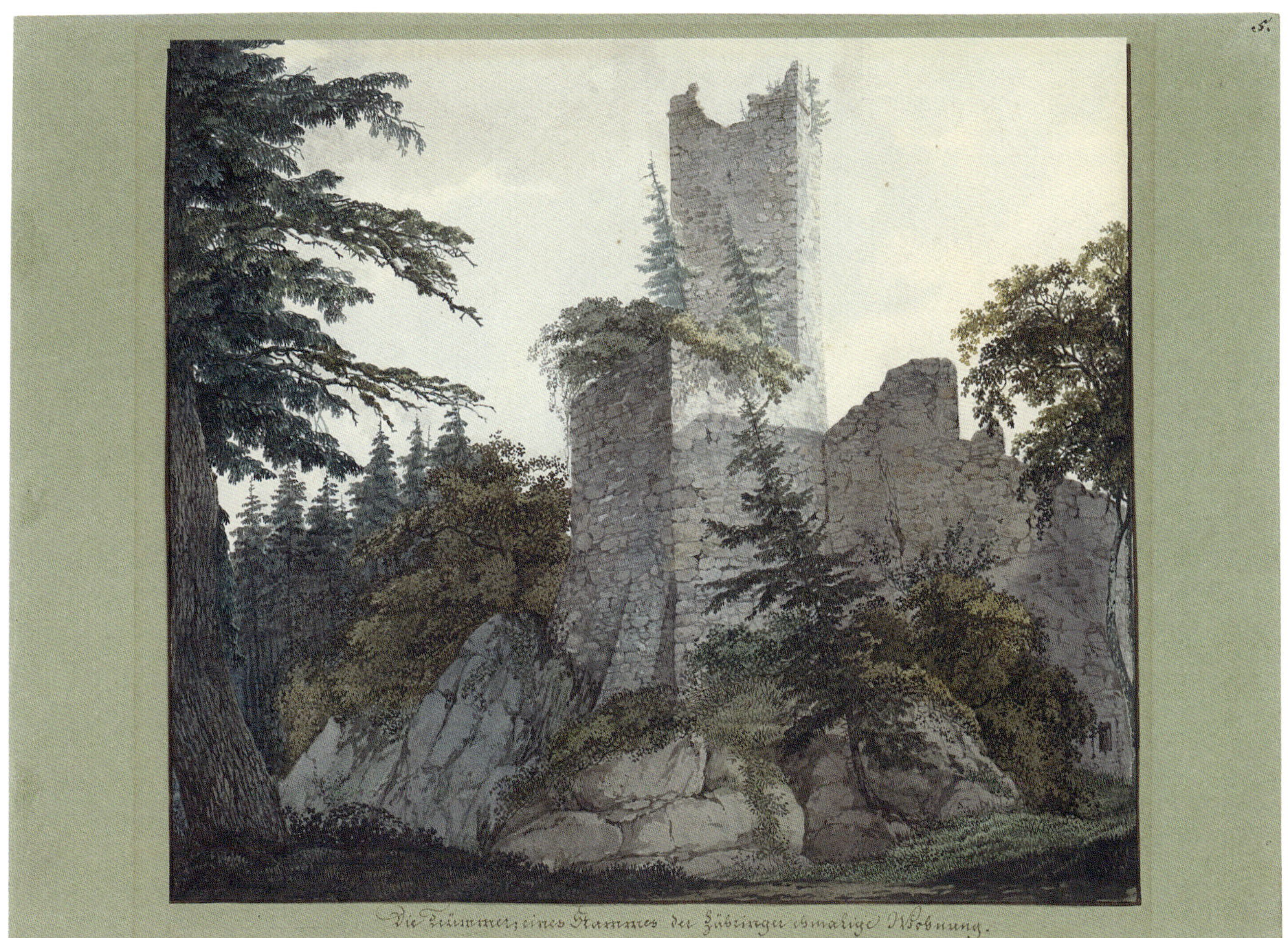

Die Trümmer; eines Stammes der Zähringer ehmalige Wohnung.

14

JOHN ROBERT COZENS

London 1752–1797 London

A ruined fort near Salerno, c. 1782

Trained by his father, Alexander (cat. 5), John Robert Cozens, in the course of a career cut short by mental illness, revolutionized the practice of watercolour in Britain. He abandoned the 'tinted drawing' of Sandby and his contemporaries, largely eschewing pencil outline and creating his compositions by applying layered washes of rich colour to the sheet.

Cozens produced the bulk of his watercolours during and after two tours of the Continent with his patrons Richard Payne Knight (1776) and William Beckford (1782); he remained in Rome for over a year following Knight's departure and may have first encountered Hackert then.[1] The present work, one of several known views of the Gulf of Salerno, was made around the time of his visit to Naples with Beckford late in 1782, as attested by a preparatory study in pencil and wash dated 8 November in an inscription. Working in his characteristically restricted palette of blue and grey, relieved only by a few touches of purple in the hillside vegetation and white opaque watercolour in the clouds, Cozens sacrificed specificity of detail in favour of establishing a sense of sombre monumentality. Scratching into the watercolour along the crests of the mountain and in the sea at its base produces a sense of texture and light, but the light serves mainly to emphasize the menacing height of the mountains and the encroaching darkness of the clouds swathing them. The resulting work is less concerned with recording the particulars of the location than with evoking a melancholy mood, very much in the spirit of the elder Cozens's insistence that landscape could be a vehicle for emotion.

In his last years, Cozens came under the care of Dr Thomas Monro, a collector and amateur artist. Turner and Girtin, as well as several of their contemporaries in the circle Monro established, received some of their training in watercolour by copying John Robert Cozens's work, carrying his achievements into the next generation of artists.

Graphite, watercolour and opaque watercolour (with scratching out) on laid paper,
251 × 368 cm
The Courtauld Gallery, Samuel Courtauld Trust, D.2007.DS.12

INSCRIPTIONS

Verso: collector's mark of John Percy (L.1504); centre, in brown ink, *In the Bay of Salerno,* below, in graphite (same hand?), *Near Salerno;* lower left, in graphite, *Exhibited at the Burlington | Fine Arts Club 1922/23 | No 29;* lower centre, in graphite (same hand), *The original Study from nature | dated 7th Nov. 1782 is in | Mr Beckford SRC/C/C Vol IV p. 17;* lower right, in graphite (different hand), *by J. R. Cozens. | 0553*

PROVENANCE

William Beckford (1760–1844); his sale, 10 April 1805, lot 64; Dr Thomas Monro (1759–1833); Dr John Percy (1817–1889); his sale, Christie's, 16 April 1890, lot 290, as *Bay of Salerno;* Frank W. Keen, by 1922; his sale, Christie's, 10 November 1933, lot 109; Smith; Frank C. Parker; Agnew's, by 1973; Dorothy Scharf (1942–2004); Scharf Bequest, 2007

NOTES

1 The two artists are known to have met in Naples during Cozens's 1782 tour with Beckford; see cat. 4.

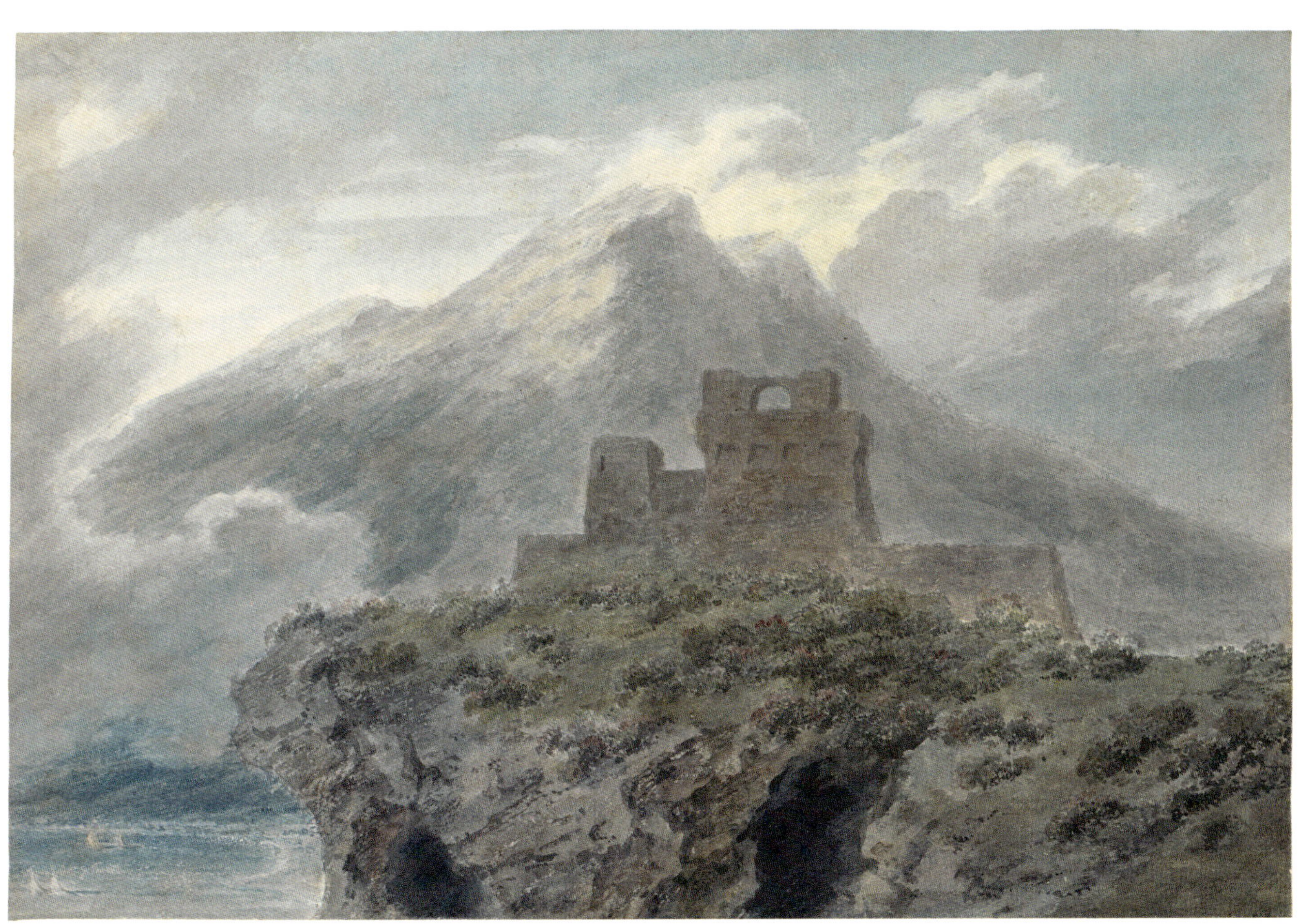

London 1805–1881 Redhill

15

Oak tree and beech, Lullingstone Park, c. 1828

In 1828, Palmer's mentor and future father-in-law John Linnell commissioned him to make drawings of trees in the park surrounding Lullingstone Castle, seat of the Hart Dyke family since 1500, near Shoreham. The present drawing is one of three such known works, all of which focus on a massive, gnarled oak.[1]

In a letter to Linnell in December 1828, Palmer described the oak in distinctly anthropomorphic terms: "... the moss, and rifts, and barky furrows, and the mouldering grey, tho' that adds majesty to the lord of forrests [sic]; mostly catch the eye before the grasp and grapple of the roots; the muscular belly and shoulders; the twisted sinews".[2] Beginning the composition in graphite and working it up in brown ink, Palmer's line ranges from the minutely descriptive, in capturing the dense textures of the knots and bulges of the oak's trunk and bark, to the exuberantly free and rapid, in the branches of the oak and the other areas of the landscape, generating an impression of controlled chaos. His use of colour is spare and non-naturalistic; areas of stippling in yellow, orange and white (some of which was added with a dry brush) – so thick they noticeably project from the sheet and given a sheen by the addition of a gum glaze – create an unearthly glow.

While Palmer's surviving 1824 sketchbook contains a number of tree studies, and a letter to Linnell written in September of that year mentions that he has "begun two studies for you on grey paper at Lullingstone", none of these earlier studies can be considered directly preparatory for this drawing. In any case, Palmer appears to have struggled with Linnell's commission, confessing to his fellow Ancient George Richmond, "Tho' I am making studies for Mr Linnell, I will, God help me, never be a naturalist by profession".[3] Despite the difficulties he experienced, the Lullingstone Park drawings represent a turning point in his art, moving away from the slightly stiff, primitivizing style, informed by medieval art, of his earlier work and towards a more direct and visionary approach to nature.

Pen and brown ink, graphite, watercolour, opaque watercolour and gum glaze on grey wove paper, 296 × 470 mm
The Morgan Library & Museum, Thaw Collection, 2006.53

INSCRIPTIONS

Recto: signed in graphite at lower left, *S Palmer fec*—. Verso: inscribed in pen and black ink at lower right, *Shoreham*.

PROVENANCE

John Linnell (1792–1882); by descent to his grandson Herbert Linnell; Mrs E.A.C. Druce; Mrs Hilda Pryor; private collection, England; sale, London, Christie's, 8 June 2000, lot 111; Eugene V. and Clare E. Thaw, New York

NOTES

1 The other two studies of trees in Lullingstone Park are in the National Gallery of Canada, Ottawa (4357) and the Yale Center for British Art, New Haven (B1977.14.308).
2 Palmer 1974, pp. 47–48.
3 Palmer 1974, p. 36.

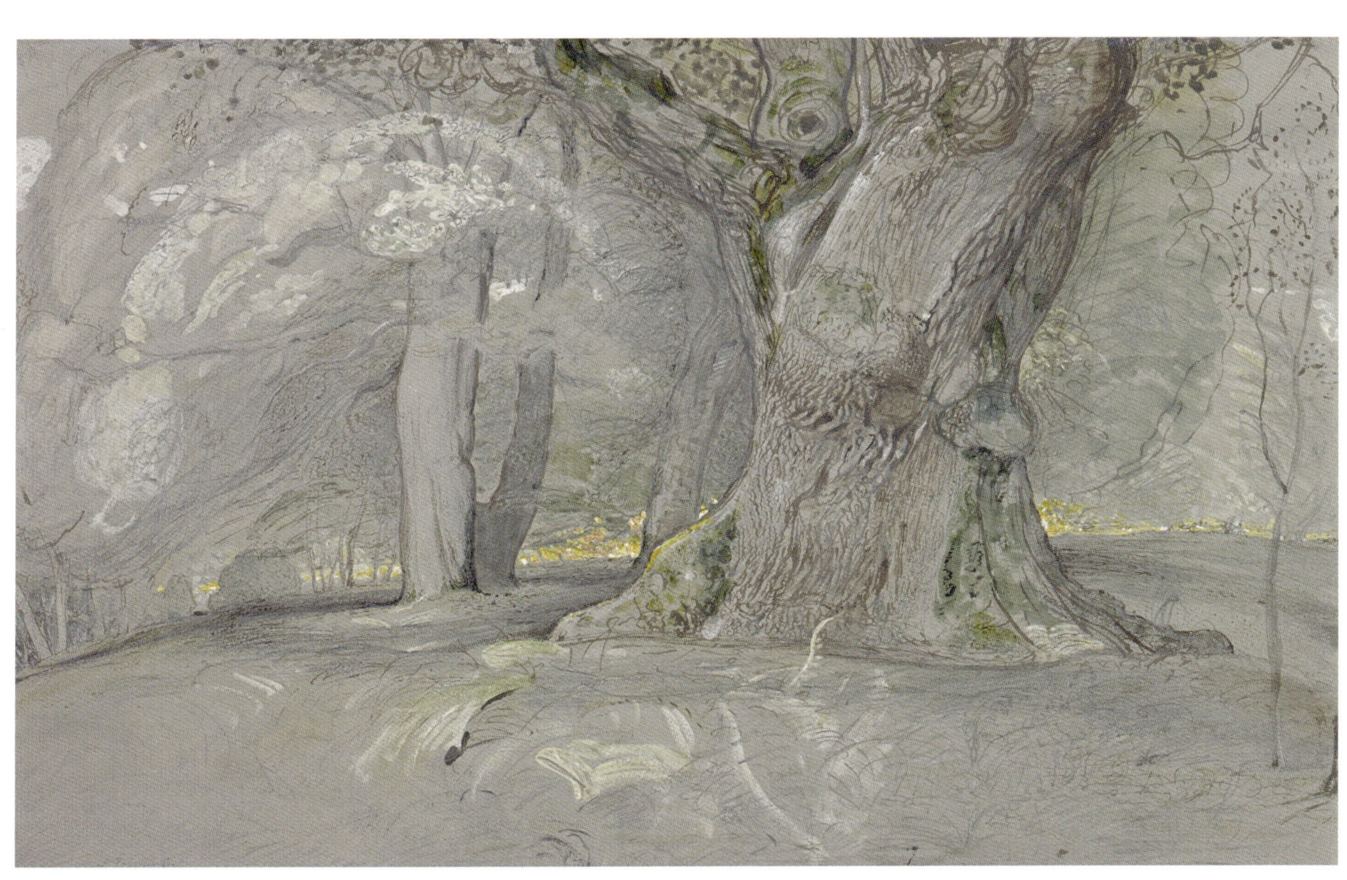

16

KARL FRIEDRICH LESSING

Breslau [Wroclaw] 1808–1880 Karlsruhe

Landscape with a cemetery and a church, 1837

Trained in Berlin, Lessing, the grandnephew of the writer and philosopher Gotthold Ephraim Lessing, was renowned during his lifetime as a history painter, and especially for a series of paintings inspired by the life of Jan Hus (c. 1369–1415). However, he was also a prolific landscapist, his early works pervaded by the influence of Jacob van Ruisdael.

The motif of an ancient or abandoned cemetery or church being overtaken by nature had occupied Lessing since the 1820s and had indeed been the subject of his first major painting, *Cemetery and ruins overtaken by trees* (Paris, Musée du Louvre, R.F. 1999–10). In contrast to the carefully finished surfaces of his paintings, the present drawing reveals the complexity of his working method. Lessing has used the bare paper (which has since darkened slightly) to create the moon, apparently scratching into the blue-grey wash surrounding it with the handle of the brush to suggest ambient light. The untouched paper is also used to represent the church walls and the gravestones, suggesting an equivalence between moon and stone and heightening the eeriness of the atmosphere. The moonlight on the tombstones, however, is rendered in white gouache, its placement determined by dramatic impact rather than a concern for realism. An irregularly shaped strip of paper has been added to the centre of the sheet, seemingly by Lessing himself, to correct an area of the composition. Another, less important, pentimento is visible in the owl at centre left, which was drawn over the branch on which it perches, visible through the bird's body.

The most striking element of the composition is the massive tree, whose gnarled trunk and twisting branches appear to be on the point of enveloping the churchyard. While Lessing's treatment of the tree is more restrained than Samuel Palmer's (cat. 15), it nonetheless exhibits the anthropomorphic qualities typical of a Romantic approach to the subject. Although, like Palmer's tree, this appears to be an oak, a tree charged with national symbolism in both Germany and Britain, with its numerous and prominent dead branches it might best be considered in this context as a reminder of mortality.

Pen and brown and black inks, brush and brown ink, brown ink wash, watercolour, opaque watercolour and graphite with cut and adhered paper correction, on brown wove paper, 291 × 447 mm
The Morgan Library & Museum, Gift of Mrs. Werner Abegg, 1984.38

INSCRIPTION

Signed lower centre in pen and brown ink, *C.F.L./März 1837*

PROVENANCE

Walter Feilchenfeldt, Zurich; Werner Abegg

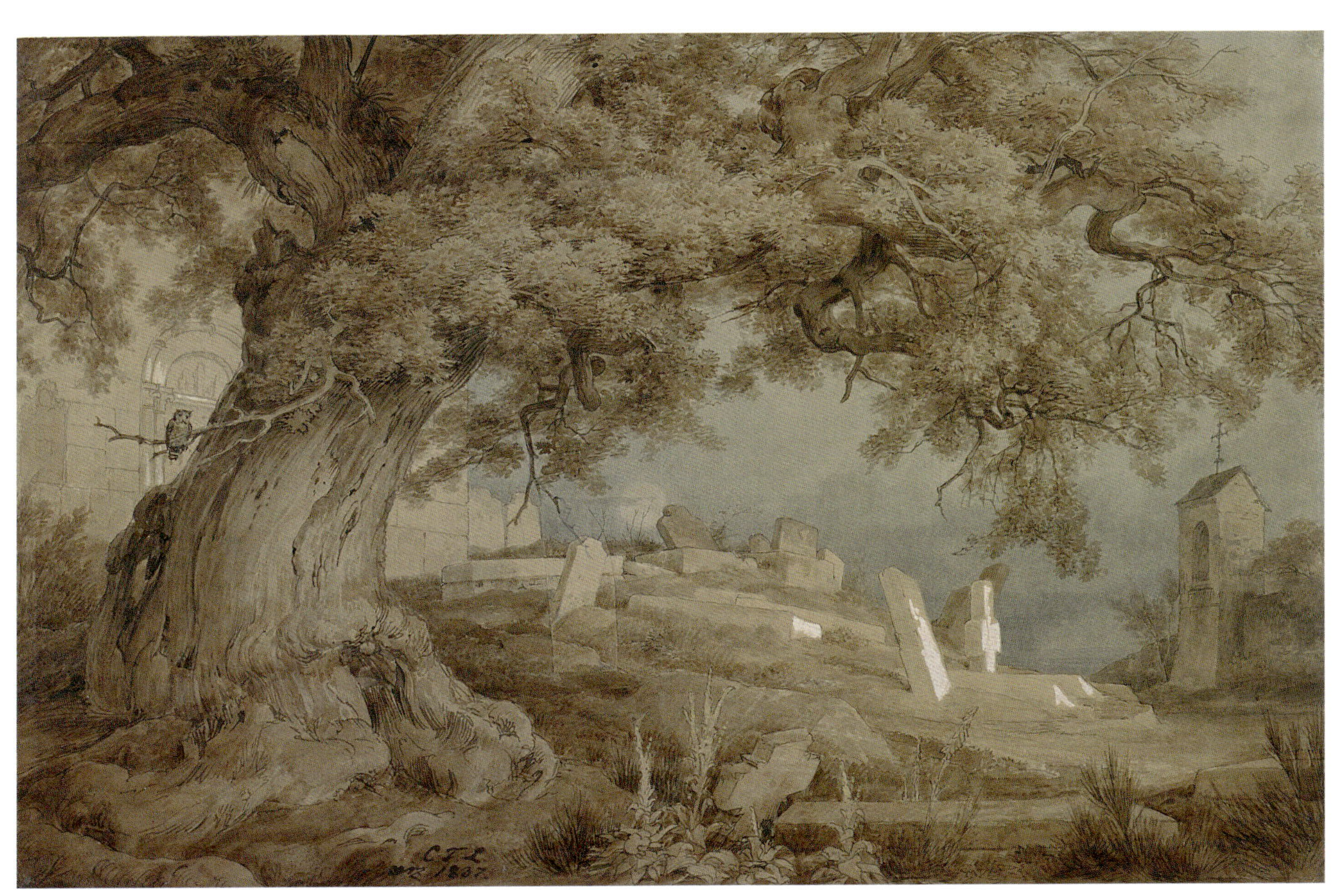

17

CASPAR DAVID FRIEDRICH

Greifswald 1774–1840 Dresden

Landscape on Rügen with shepherds and flocks, c. 1809/1810?

The Baltic island of Rügen was a place of frequent pilgrimage for Friedrich; he is documented as having visited in 1801, 1806, 1818 and 1826. The earlier visits proved particularly fertile for his work, as numerous sketches attest. Although none of the known studies relates directly to the present drawing, the gently rolling pastoral landscape depicted here – identified as a view over the Goor and Kollhof woods toward the offshore island of Vilm – is likely to have been made in the studio, based upon such an on-site drawing.

As Helmut Börsch-Supan has observed, Friedrich's first visits to Rügen occasioned a compositional breakthrough: he began to abandon conventional framing devices in favour of visions of boundless space.[1] The present drawing's composition, while not on the same vast scale of several other finished Rügen drawings, bears this out: although foreground, middle ground and background are demarcated by discrete motifs (rolling hills, a cottage nestled among trees, distant cliffs), the horizon line is low and their forms are dwarfed by the open sky, which is rendered with extraordinarily subtle and delicate washes (particularly well preserved in the present work), the wispy clouds denoted with the faintest of graphite lines. Even the archetypal Romantic motif of a blasted tree with a lichen-encrusted trunk in the lower right foreground is depicted on as diminutive a scale as the other elements of the composition.

As an island at the outer reaches of German territory, isolated, bleak and dotted with prehistoric sites, Rügen had a particular resonance for the Romantic imagination and nascent notions of national identity. All of these factors entwined in Friedrich's representations of the island, but one other decisive influence on his Rügen landscapes was his acquaintance with the local poet and pastor Gotthard Ludwig Kosegarten, whose sermons, delivered to his congregation out of doors, stressed God's presence in nature. The tiny shepherd and his flock in the middle ground might be considered a metaphor for the pastor and his congregation or perhaps even for Christ as shepherd.[2]

Pen and black ink, brown ink wash, graphite, and opaque white watercolour on wove paper; black ink lines along edges, 245 × 325 mm
The Morgan Library & Museum, Thaw Collection

INSCRIPTION

On the verso, in graphite, indications for mounting the drawing, *Ein Passep.* [Passepartout] *A mit Rückpappe*; two more lines now illegible because partly erased and, at lower left, *C.D. Friedrich*

PROVENANCE

Private collection or art market, Weimar, before 1945; private collection, Berlin; C.G. Boerner, Düsseldorf; Seiden & de Cuevas, New York; Eugene V. and Clare E. Thaw, New York

NOTES

1 Börsch-Supan 1960, pp. 65–76.
2 On Friedrich's relationship with Kosegarten, see Koerner 2009, pp. 94–97.

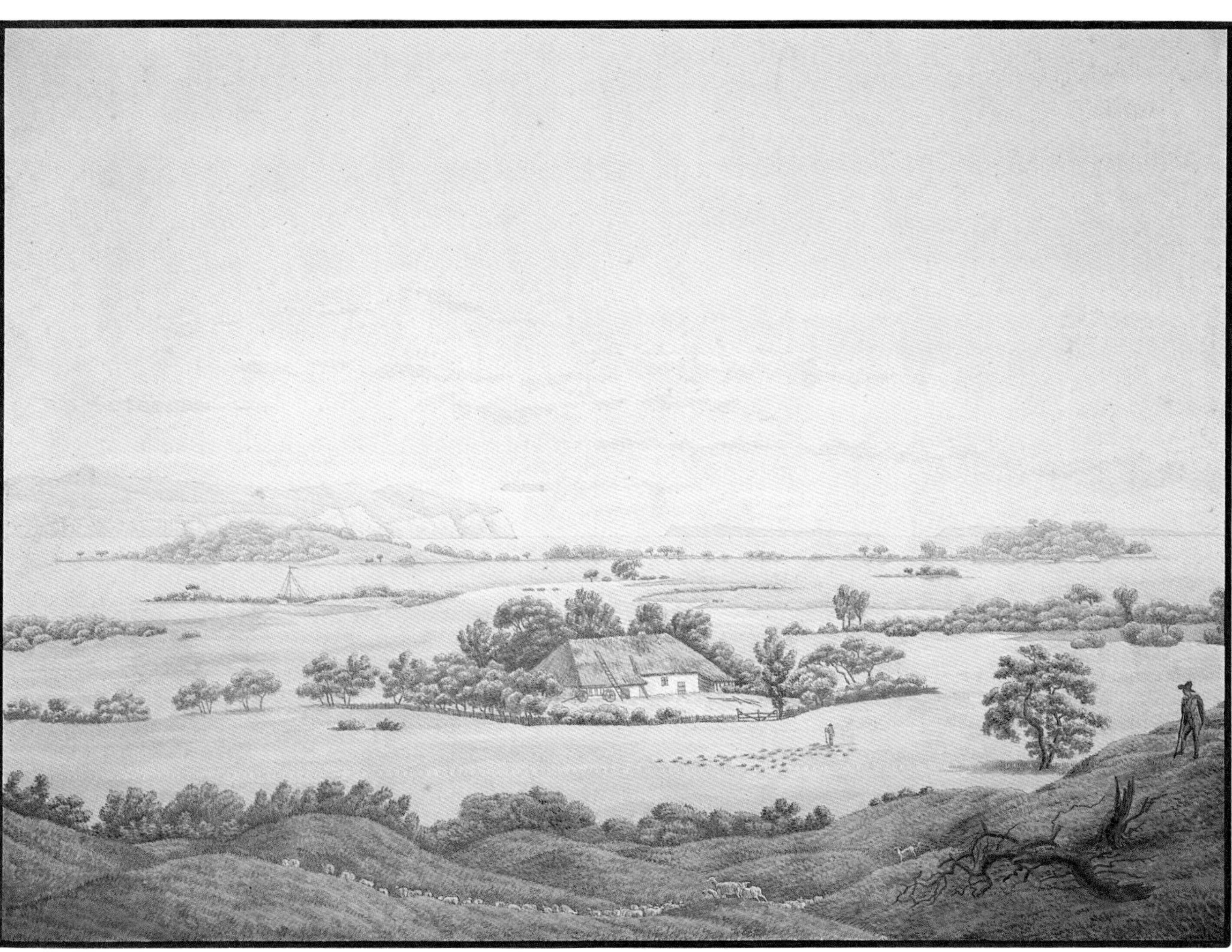

18

THOMAS GIRTIN

London 1775–1802 London

Near Kelso, c. 1800–01

Turner's exact contemporary, Girtin began his career as a topographical draughtsman under the tutelage of Edward Dayes (1763–1804). From 1794, he and Turner began to frequent the house of the amateur Dr Thomas Monro, where exposure to the work of John Robert Cozens began to effect a shift in Girtin's approach from the tinted drawings of his previous master toward a freer, more painterly style.

Girtin made two tours of the Scottish Borders over the course of his brief career. This view of the River Tweed near Kelso is one of four known depictions of the area made during or shortly after his second trip in the summer of 1800.[1] The vista depicted in the present work is probably taken either from the town's bridge or from a ferry anchored mid-river, looking upstream toward the confluence of the Tweed and the Teviot.[2] This broad expanse of water allowed Girtin to create an implicit panoramic effect, even within the confines of a sheet of standard proportions. This sense of breadth extends to the handling: scarcely any graphite underdrawing is visible, and the forms are delineated in broad washes of Girtin's preferred palette of blues, greys and browns; foreground details are denoted with his characteristic dots and vigorous dashes of dark brown ink, probably applied with a reed pen. Girtin also largely abandoned traditional framing devices – the river stretches unbroken to both sides of the sheet, and the clump of trees in the middle ground directs the eye into the scene and beyond. This, in combination with his division of the composition into bands of water, land and sky and his treatment of the landscape as an arrangement of masses of light and dark colour, gives rise to a sense of endless space similar to Friedrich's nearly contemporaneous compositional experiments on Rügen (of which Girtin is unlikely to have known), imbuing an otherwise unspectacular landscape with a feeling of breadth and grandeur.

Graphite, pen and ink and watercolour on laid paper, 260 × 438 mm
The Courtauld Gallery, Samuel Courtauld Trust, D.2007.DS.18

INSCRIPTION

Signed, lower left, *Girtin*

WATERMARK

S

PROVENANCE

Thomas Calvert Girtin; Mrs Rogge; C. Morland Agnew; Vice-Admiral Sir William Agnew; Dorothy Scharf (1942–2004); Scharf Bequest, 2007

NOTES

1 Girtin and Loshak 1954, nos. 488–91.
2 I am grateful to Greg Smith for identifying the location as well as confirming the date of the work (email correspondence, 8 June 2010 and 25 June 2013).

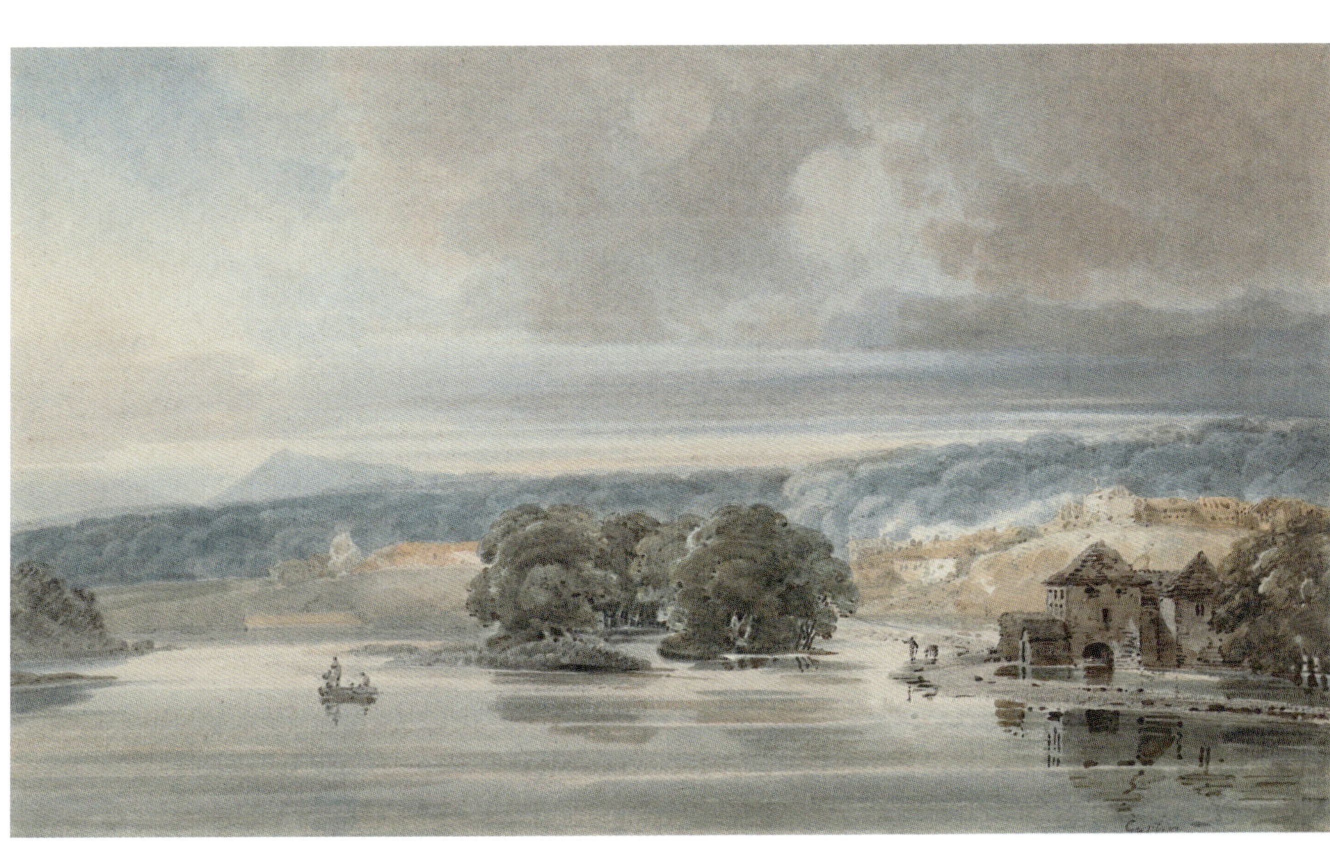

19

JOSEPH MALLORD WILLIAM TURNER
London 1775–1851 London

Mont Blanc, from above Courmayeur, c. 1810

Thanks to the short-lived Peace of Amiens, Turner was able to visit the Continent for the first time in 1802. Between mid July and October he journeyed through France to Savoy, also visiting the Val d'Aosta and parts of Switzerland; he was among the first major British artists to tour the Val d'Aosta. He had previously known the spectacular Alpine landscapes through the works of John Robert Cozens. In person he considered the Alps, with typical understatement, "on the whole [to surpass] Wales", and they obviously captured his imagination; he filled three sketchbooks over the course of the journey with pencil sketches of the mountains and valleys.[1]

The present work, which depicts Mont Blanc from above the village of Courmayeur at an angle that discloses the entrance to Val Veni with the Brenva Glacier spilling down the mountainside, is one of two finished watercolours Turner developed from his on-the-spot sketches.[2] The gap of about eight years between the sketch – which contains no colour notes – and the finished watercolour implies that he relied on a combination of memory and imagination for the luminous colour and rich textural effects. Although he adhered fairly closely to the composition of the sketch, he simplified the contours of the mountains and exaggerated their height to emphasize the magnificence of the view. The mountains in the middle ground and the wooded banks of the stream in the foreground are rendered in subtle layers of colours, with blue-green (now faded) brushed over reddish brown to conjure both shadows and vegetation. Extensive scraping out and drawing in the wet watercolour, probably with the end of the brush, further heighten the contrast between the dark contours of the valley entrance and the ethereal quality of the snow-covered Mont Blanc, which appears to dissolve into the clouds, evoking a feeling of infinite space. Through means strikingly different to those used fifteen years later by Oehme (cat. 21), Turner evokes the grandeur of the Alps and, by way of the minutely rendered figures and buildings, the contrast between the tranquil but fragile human landscape and the awe-inspiring mountains.

Watercolour (applied in washes and with the point of a brush) and graphite, some drawing into the wet paint with a sharp point and extensive scraping out, on white wove drawing cartridge paper, 282 × 398 mm
The Courtauld Gallery, Samuel Courtauld Trust, D.1974.STC.6

PROVENANCE

Sir William Pilkington; John Dillon; his sale, Christie's, 17 April 1869, lot 44, as *Mont Blanc from Aosta*, bought in; J.F. Haworth, by 1918; Agnew's, 1918, as *Valley of Aosta, with Mont Blanc in the Distance*, c. 1810; Sir Stephen Courtauld, 1919; Gift in memory of Sir Stephen Courtauld, 1974

NOTES

1 Farington 1978–84, vol. 5 (1979), p. 1890. The sketchbooks in question are part of the Turner Bequest, London, Tate (nos. LXXIII, LXXIV and LXXV).
2 The sketches from which both watercolours evolved are TB LXXIII 66v–67r and 67v–68r. The second Courmayeur watercolour is *Saint Hugues denouncing vengeance on the shepherd of Cormayeur, in the valley of d'Aoust*, exhibited at the Royal Academy in 1803 (now in the collection of Sir John Soane's Museum, London).

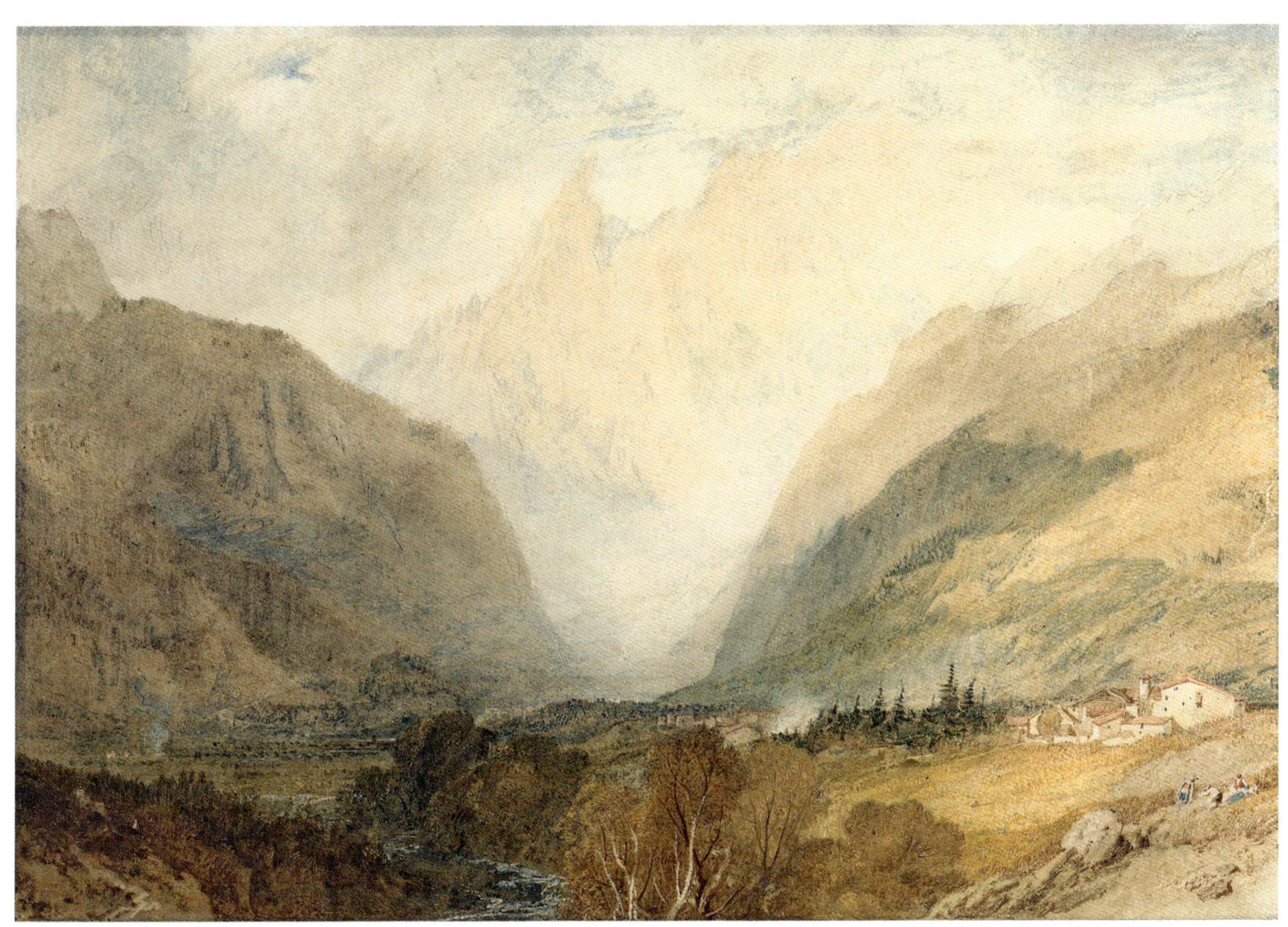

20

Sankt Goarshausen and Katz Castle, 1817

Turner's first trip to the Continent following the end of the Napoleonic Wars was also his first visit to Germany: starting from Cologne, he travelled along the Rhine to Mainz and back. His choice may have been informed by Lord Byron's *Childe Harold's Pilgrimage* (1816), whose third canto contains lyrical descriptions of the Rhineland scenery through which Turner travelled the following year.[1]

This watercolour, which depicts a stretch of the river as it passes between cliffs downstream from Sankt Goarshausen, is one of a group of fifty recording Turner's Rhine journey which he sold to his patron Walter Fawkes upon his return. In the middle distance, illuminated by the setting sun, is the ruined fourteenth-century castle of Neukatzenelnbogen, known as 'Burg Katz' – not an ancient ruin, but a recent casualty of war, blown up by Napoleon's troops in 1806. Although the picturesque ruins must have appealed to Turner's sensibilities, they are likely also to have served as a reminder of the wars that had riven Germany.

As with most of his Rhine watercolours, Turner prepared the paper with a pale grey wash, giving the subsequent layers of watercolour a cool, silvery tone. The surface of the drawing is more heavily worked than it is in many of the other Rhine works, with extensive scraping in the cliff faces and ribbon-like streaks of white opaque watercolour added to the water's surface to indicate reflections, and the palette richer and warmer. Scholars have tended to assume that Turner produced most of the Rhine watercolours after returning to Britain, working from the three sketchbooks he filled on the trip. Although the present work is known to be based on a pencil sketch in the Waterloo and Rhine sketchbook (Tate, TB CLX 75v), the existence of several other views of the environs of Sankt Goarshausen depicted at different times of day has led David Hill to suggest that they might have been coloured on the spot.[2] In either case, this watercolour and its companions strongly convey Turner's enthusiastic response to the German landscape, while their somewhat sketch-like appearance appears to presage the ever more open quality of Turner's late watercolours (see cat. 22).

Watercolour (applied in washes and with the point of a brush) and white opaque watercolour (with scraping) and graphite on wove paper, trimmed and prepared with a grey wash, 196 × 307 mm
The Courtauld Gallery, Samuel Courtauld Trust, D.1974.STC.10

PROVENANCE

Walter Fawkes; by descent to Revd Ayscough Fawkes; his sale, Christie's, 27 June 1890, lot 10; Vokins; Christie's, 20 March 1896, lot 178; G.R. Burnett; his sale, Christie's, 21 March 1908, lot 27; Agnew; W.G. Rawlinson, 1908; T.A. Tatton; Christie's, 12–14 December 1928, lot 16; A.J. Finberg; Cotswold Gallery, 1930; Sir Stephen Courtauld; Gift in memory of Sir Stephen Courtauld, 1974

Exhibited in London only

NOTES

1   For a comprehensive account of Turner's 1817 Rhine tour, see London 1994, pp. 20–29.
2   Hill 2003, p. 11.

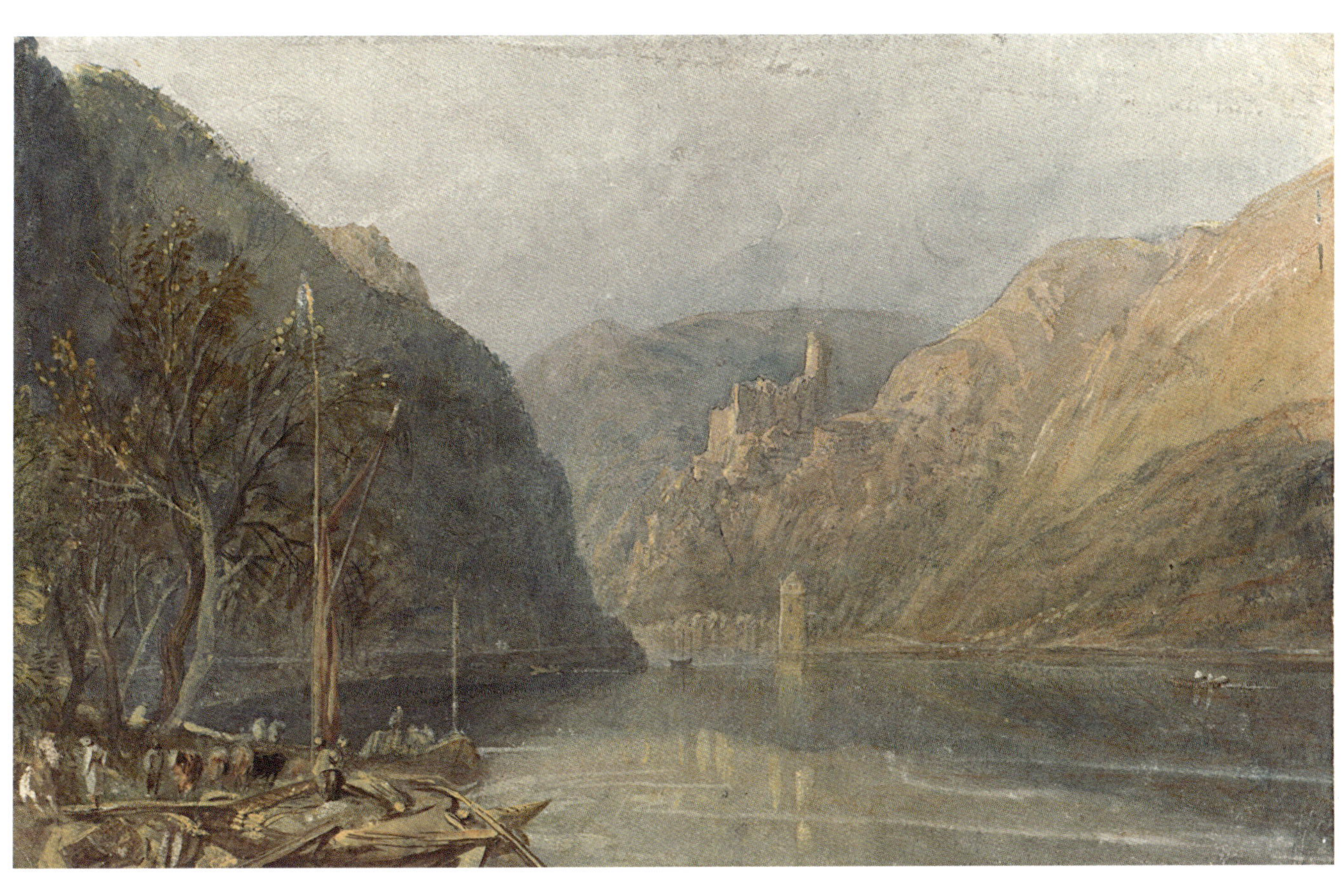

21

ERNST FERDINAND OEHME

Dresden 1797–1855 Dresden

View in the Alps, 1825

The Dresden-born Oehme, who studied under Friedrich and was also mentored by Dahl, travelled to Rome in 1822, where he spent three years. The return journey through the Alps in 1825 inspired this watercolour, one of seven known Alpine views that originated during his travels.[1] All executed on sheets of the same size, these highly finished drawings do not relate directly to any paintings in Oehme's oeuvre and may be considered autonomous works of art.

One of the related Alpine watercolours, *Burg Naudersberg in Tirol* (Cologne, Wallraf-Richartz-Museum) provides an insight into Oehme's working method.[2] He seems to have sketched the main outlines first, in graphite, possibly on the spot, further working them up in pen and ink. Colour, in the form of monochrome washes, watercolour and white gouache, was added in the studio, along with further penwork to define the foreground vegetation. The gap of several months between viewing the landscape and committing it to paper may account for the abstract quality of the colour, which is laid on in broad, transparent washes, firmly contained by the pen outlines. An analogous approach may be seen in the watercolours of Francis Towne (cat. 10), who made a similar journey in 1780–81, although it is unlikely that Oehme would have been aware of the older artist's work.

Although the crystalline quality of Oehme's rendering of the Alpine landscape differs sharply from the more painterly technique of contemporaries such as Turner, his chosen subject-matter places him firmly within a Romantic approach to landscape. The viewpoint and the brilliant white peaks in the background create a sense of panoramic splendour while the beetling mountains in the middle ground suggest man's insignificance in the face of nature. This sensation is heightened by the absence of figures; a human presence is indicated only by the pump and trough in the foreground and the fenced path leading the eye toward an isolated mountain hut.

Watercolour, opaque watercolour, pen and black ink and graphite, on wove paper, 236 × 334 mm
The Morgan Library & Museum, purchased as the gift of Catherine Mellon Conover, 1986.14

WATERMARK

J WHATMAN // TURKEY MILL // 181[?] (last number of year illegible)

INSCRIPTIONS

Lower centre in light brown ink, [illegible]; at lower right, . . .g[?]*au* and *Schutzengelhorner* [?]; on verso, at lower centre in graphite, by a later hand, *1825 auf der Reise nach Italien gez*; at upper centre, *Ernst Oehme*

PROVENANCE

Galerie Arnoldi-Livie, Munich

Exhibited in New York only

NOTES

1   The other Alpine watercolours of 1825 include *Burg Naudersberg in Tirol* (Cologne, Wallraf-Richartz-Museum); *The Pianazzo Waterfall, The Rigi* and *Evening in the Tyrolean Alps near Niedendorf* (Dresden, Kupferstichkabinett); and *The Wetterhorn with the Rosenlaui Glacier from the Scheidegg* (Berlin, Kupferstichkabinett).
2   Cologne 1986, no. 85, p. 184.

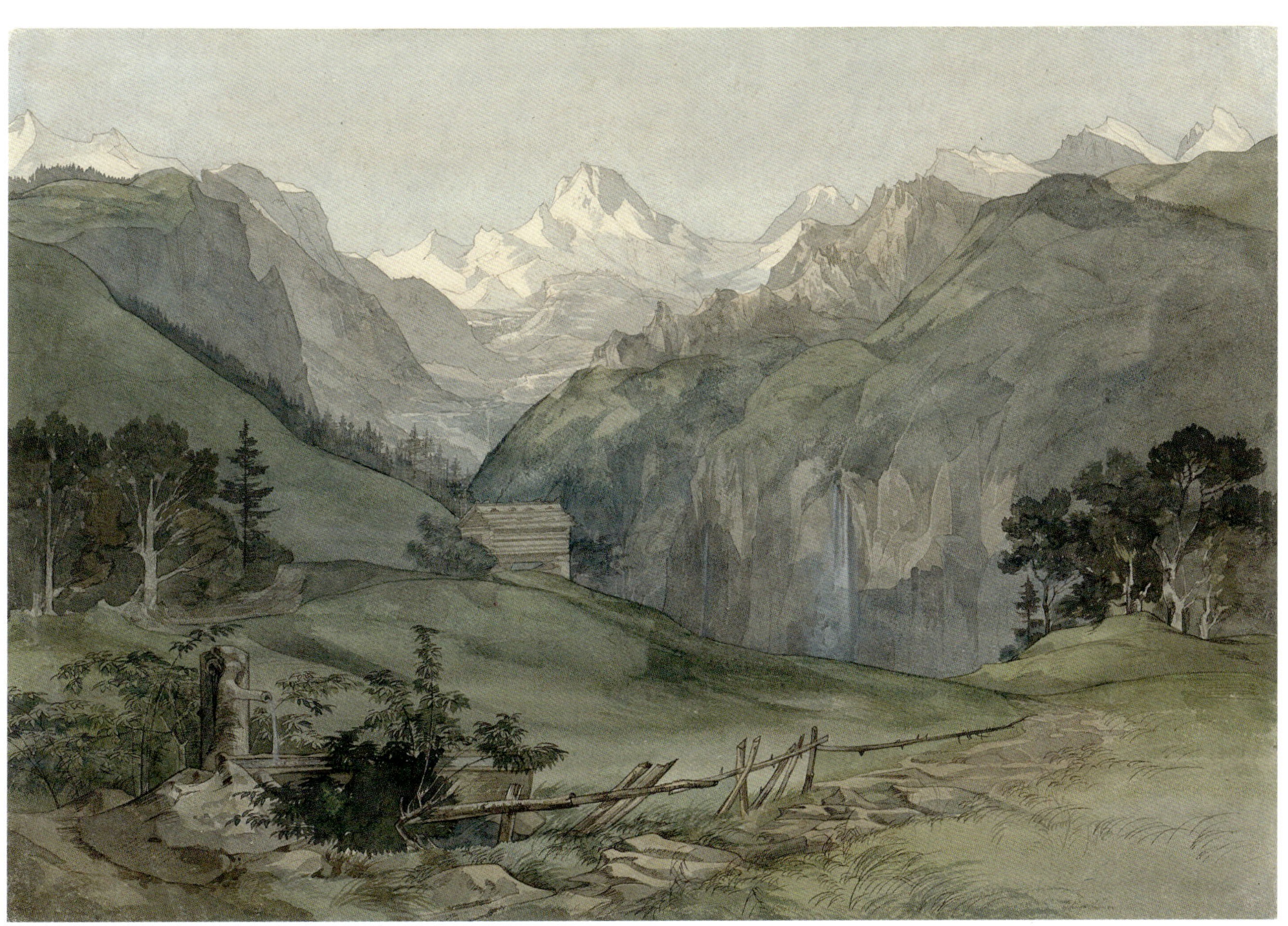

22

CASPAR DAVID FRIEDRICH

Greifswald 1774–1840 Dresden

Moonlit landscape, before 1808?

The moon figures prominently in Friedrich's art, but this luminous watercolour, in which a full moon floats above a pond in a clearing in the woods is unusual in that the moon is formed by a piece of blank paper inserted behind a hole cut in the sheet. The watercolour is likely a 'transparent', that is, a drawing intended to be illuminated from behind.[1] Candlelight filtering through the unpainted paper would have made the moon the brightest point in the composition (an effect amplified by the delicate stippling and apparent scratching into the watercolour around the moon), casting a palpable glow over the scene.

Friedrich's other moonlit landscapes, such as *Two men contemplating the moon* (1819, Dresden, Gemäldegalerie), usually focus on the communion between man and nature. Here, the only sign of human presence is a statue, possibly a Mater Dolorosa but whose identity is ultimately unclear (what appears to be a sword in its breast may in fact be a cross). Friedrich appears to make an explicit connection between the moon and God or Christ; its function as a transmitter of light is analogous to Christ's role as intermediary between God and mankind. It has been suggested that the statue and broken tree-trunk at left represent the death of Christ and the moon and birch tree, his resurrection.

Friedrich's other 'transparents', commissioned by his patron Vasily Zhukovskii, were intended to be viewed by lamplight in a darkened room, accompanied by music. Because of its apparent relation to Zhukovskii's commission, the present drawing has been tentatively dated to 1830–35;[2] however, the existence of a study for the trees and fence at left (Oslo, Nasjonalgalleriet, NG.K&H.B.16007) dated 23 October 1801, and family documents indicating that Friedrich had given the drawing to his sister, Catherina Sponholz, who died in 1808, suggest that it may have been created earlier,[3] thus raising the possibility that a search for new ways to represent moonlight had occupied Friedrich for the better part of his career. This concern places him at the heart of Romantic experiments with representing light that go back to Turner's early 'transparent' watercolours of the 1790s and to Gainsborough.[4]

Watercolour and opaque watercolour on wove paper; moon cut out and inserted on a separate piece of paper; laid down on cardboard, 232 × 365 mm
The Morgan Library & Museum, Thaw Collection, 1996.150

PROVENANCE

Catherina Dorothea Sponholz (1766–1808), the artist's sister; Caroline Sponholz, the artist's niece; F. Pflugradt, Zingst (a descendant of the Sponholz family; until 1941); Galerie Meissner, Zurich; Eugene V. and Clare E. Thaw, New York

Exhibited in London only

NOTES

1 The drawing was first described as such in Börsch-Supan and Jähnig 1973, no. 440.
2 Ibid.
3 Sabine Rewald notes that it was not unusual for Friedrich to reuse drawings as a source for watercolours and paintings even after a gap of thirty years (New York 2001, no. 9).
4 Turner is known to have produced at least eight such 'transparents', the earliest dated one of which is *Chepstow Castle* of 1793 (Courtauld Gallery, D.1974.STC.1).

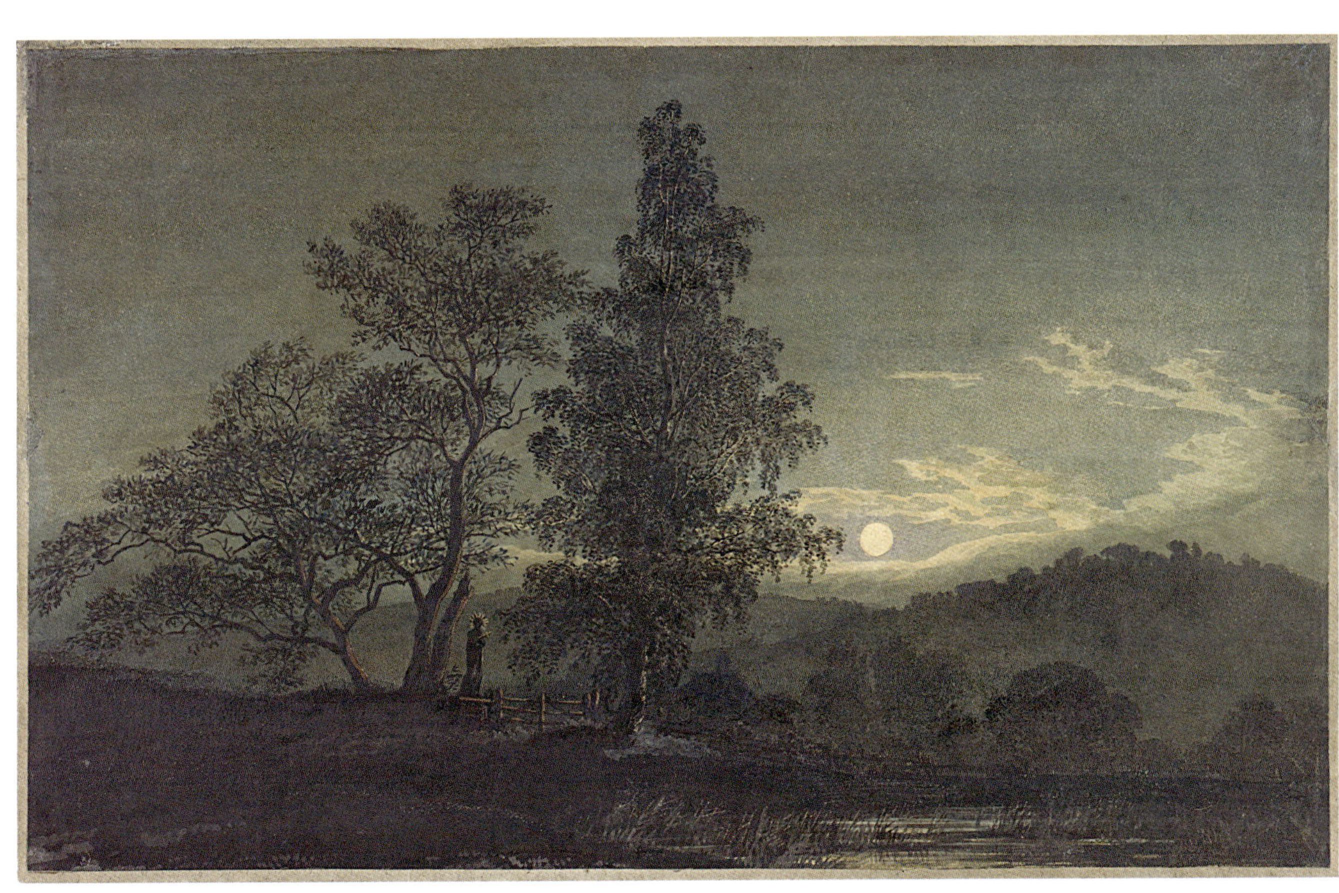

23

JOSEPH MALLORD WILLIAM TURNER

London 1775–1851 London

On Lake Lucerne, looking towards Fluelen, c. 1841?

By the early 1840s – by which time he had become an inveterate Continental traveller – Turner's approach to landscape had undergone radical changes. He rejected the topographical specificity of his earlier work and sought instead – particularly in a remarkable group of watercolours resulting from his 1841 tour of Switzerland – to capture effects of light and atmosphere.

The present work exemplifies this major shift in Turner's approach; the identity of the site depicted has been the subject of lengthy debate (at one point in its history, it was even thought to represent an island off the coast of Scotland) and has only recently been confirmed as a view of Lake Lucerne looking south along the Bay of Uri towards Fluelen.[1] The mountains that ring the lake are here reduced to a single rocky promontory, its contours and that of the shoreline delineated by a single faint graphite line. The rest of the land is dissolved in veils of grey mist through which the light of a full moon filters onto the water, its surface lightly ruffled by a breeze. The full moon, indicated by a circle of white gouache, exerts a powerful physical presence despite being half-covered by mist. By superimposing translucent washes and employing a wide range of effects – dragged dry brushstrokes to evoke moonlight veiled by the mist, scratching into the paper and smudging the watercolour with his fingers to suggest gradations of colour in the sky – Turner vividly and subtly renders the elusive effects of moonlight.

Although the mood of calm intensity evoked by the all-pervading blue tonality has been associated with Turner's response to Goethe's colour theories (which had recently been translated into English),[2] the loose, atmospheric brushwork suggests the extent to which British and German Romantic approaches to landscape had diverged by the 1840s. While the minute brushwork, meticulous detail and religious symbolism of Friedrich's earlier *Moonlit landscape* (cat. 22) may at first glance appear alien to Turner's approach, the visionary intensity of both artists' treatment of the moon suggests a common concern, explored through markedly different avenues.

Watercolour, with scraping out and marks made with the thumb, over graphite on wove paper, 223 × 283 mm
The Courtauld Gallery, Samuel Courtauld Trust, D.2007.DS.47

INSCRIPTIONS

Verso: in graphite, upper left, '1317'

PROVENANCE

Henry Vaughan; Louis Huth; his sale, Christie's, 20 May 1905 (lot 23, as *The Bass Rock – Moonlight*); Agnew's; W. G. Rawlinson, 1906; Agnew's, 1917 (as *The Seelisberg, Lake of Lucerne: Moonlight*); Reginald A. Tatton, 1917; by descent to T. A. Tatton; Christie's, 14 December 1928 (lot 31, as *The Seelisberg, Lake of Lucerne*); Agnew's; Landon K. Thorne, 1936; by descent to Mrs A. B. Thorne (by 1972); Agnew's, 1972; private collection, 1973; Agnew's, 1976; Dorothy Scharf (1942–2004), 1976; Scharf Bequest, 2007

NOTES

1   The view was identified by Joanna Selborne and confirmed by Ian Warrell in 2008; see London 2008, p. 102.
2   On Turner's reading of Goethe, see Gage 1969, pp. 173–88. Goethe associated blue with passivity, contemplation and melancholy (see Eastlake 1967 (first published 1840), pp. 310–12).

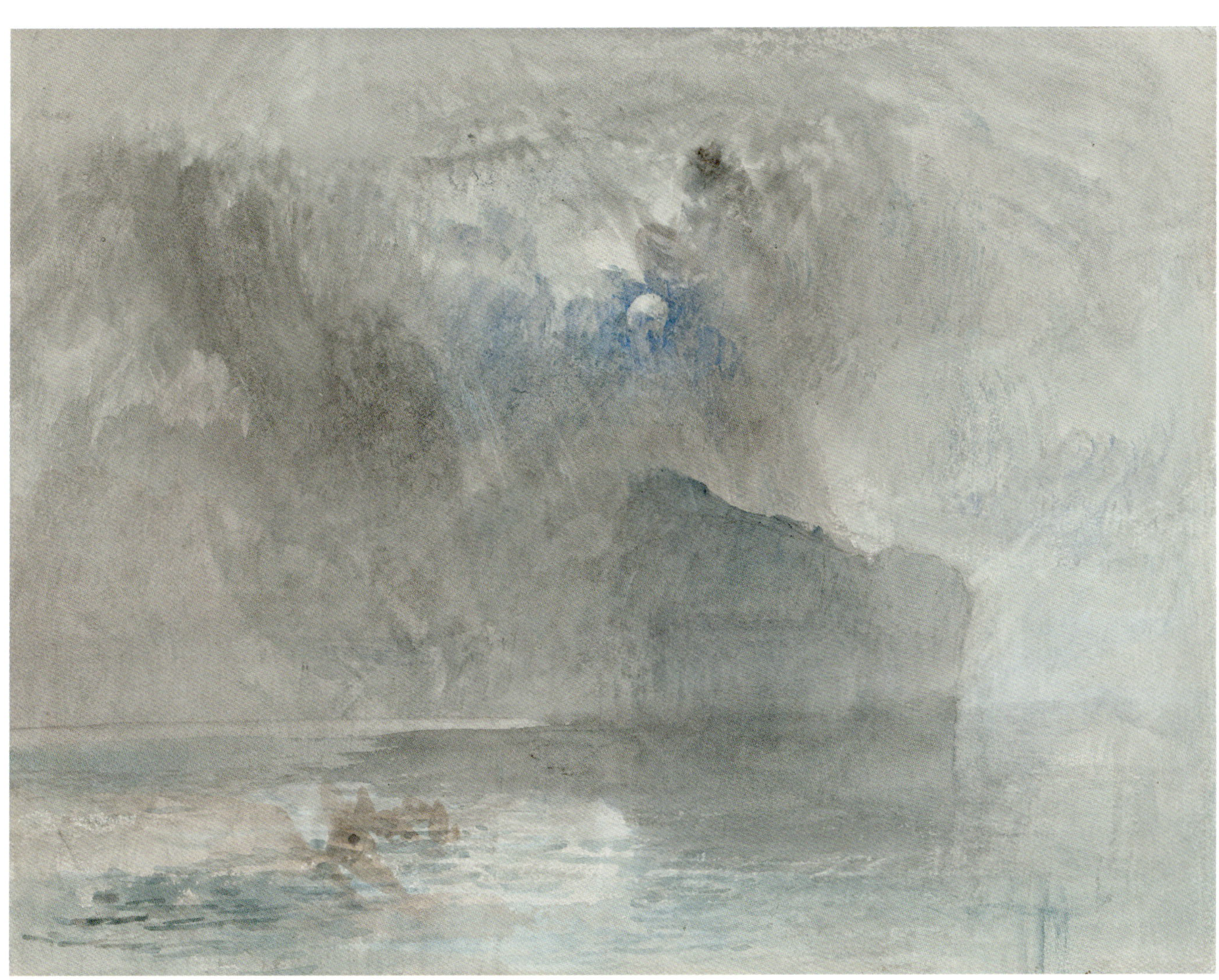

24

THEODOR REHBENITZ

Borstel 1791–1861 Kiel

Fantastic landscape with monk crossing a bridge, c. 1826–30

Rehbenitz, whose studies in Vienna (1813–16) brought him into contact with Caspar David Friedrich and two future members of the Nazarenes, Julius Schnorr von Carolsfeld (1794–1872) and Ferdinand Olivier (1785–1841), spent the first two decades of his career in Italy. In Rome he joined the Capitolines, the Protestant counterpart of the Catholic Nazarenes; both groups sought a return to what they perceived as the purity and simplicity of early German art. He worked almost exclusively as a draughtsman, leaving only a handful of oil paintings but a large body of drawings.

The subject-matter and draughtsmanship of this exceptionally refined and profusely detailed fantasy landscape suggest a date in the late 1820s, when Rehbenitz was living in Rome and Perugia.[1] The drawing is characterized by an extremely fine line and close hatching, recalling the engravings of Albrecht Dürer – a touchstone not only for the Nazarenes but also for the English Ancients, especially Samuel Palmer (see cat. 15 and 25). Rehbenitz has, however, diminished the drawing's resemblance to an engraving through the sparing use of brown ink in a few carefully chosen areas, such as the shadowy understory of the woods at centre left and the roofline of the chapel, lending warmth and depth to the image. The architecture may have been based, in a general sense, upon buildings Rehbenitz encountered on his travels in Italy, especially in Umbria, but the stylized, deliberately archaic forms of the mountain range and the mushroom- and umbrella-shaped trees suggest a work primarily inspired by the art of the Italian 'Primitives', particularly Fra Angelico, and Rehbenitz's own imagination. The synthesis of these diverse elements through Rehbenitz's delicate draughtsmanship gives rise to a sense of dreamlike enchantment at a great remove from mundane reality.

Pen and black and brown inks, on laid paper, 168 × 149 mm
The Morgan Library & Museum, Bequest of Charles Ryskamp, 2010.82

WATERMARK

Partial watermark with initials JH & Z

INSCRIPTION

On verso, *Ramboux*

PROVENANCE

Baron Carl Friedrich von Rumohr; August Grahl; C. Henmann; possibly Paul Arndt, Munich; his sale, Leipzig, C.G. Boerner, 16 May 1934, no. 295, pl. XIII; Baskett & Day Ltd, London; Charles Ryskamp; Bequest of Charles Ryskamp, 2010

NOTE

1 See Wolf-Timm 1991, nos. 665–76.

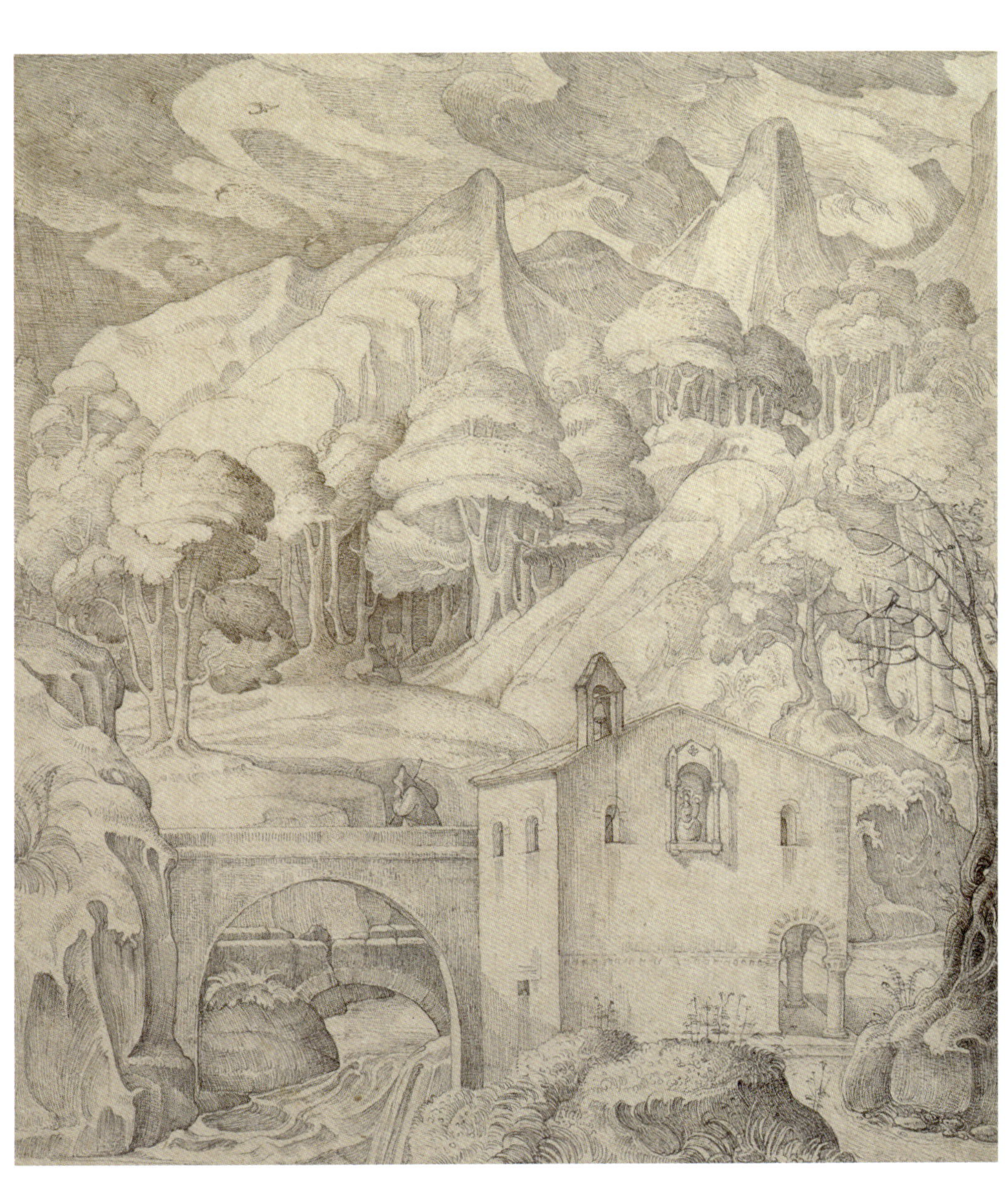

London 1805–1881 Redhill

25

The Haunted Stream, c. 1826

Typical of the drawings Palmer made shortly after he moved to
Shoreham,[1] this small wash drawing takes its title and its subject of
poetic meditation in nature from a couplet from Milton's *L'Allegro*
[The Cheerful Man] (ii, 129–30):

> *Such sights as youthful poets dream*
> *On summer eves by haunted stream.*

Milton's poetry served as a major source of inspiration to Palmer
and his fellow Ancients. While the site depicted in the drawing has been
identified as a rise above Shoreham with the hills of the Darent River
valley visible in the background, Palmer's primary concern seems to
have been less with topographical specificity than with the evocation
of a poetic, contemplative mood. Without the constraints imposed by
extensive formal training, Palmer's technique was novel; the trees here
offer an early example of the stippling that would become characteristic
of his Shoreham work, while the reflection of the chapel in the stream
seems to have been created by dragging a dry brush vertically over the
wash. The bare paper is used to form the crescent moon, the stars and
the reflections of light on the water.

The drawing's diminutive scale and delicate handling and the
lacelike structure of the Gothic chapel observed by the figure on the
riverbank all point to Palmer's engagement with the prints of earlier
northern artists, principally Albrecht Dürer and Lucas van Leyden, in
which he had been encouraged by his mentor, John Linnell. It is likely
that Palmer was also aware of the parallel, slightly earlier enthusiasm
of the Nazarenes for German Renaissance art.[2]

Brush and brown ink and brown ink wash
on wove paper, 92 × 123 mm
The Morgan Library & Museum, Thaw
Collection

PROVENANCE

A.H. Palmer; Mrs. George A. Martin, Cleveland,
Ohio; Mr. and Mrs. Alfred Barr, Jr., New York;
Eugene V. and Clare E. Thaw, New York

Exhibited in London only

NOTES

1   Scholars differ as to the dating of the
    drawing. Raymond Lister places the drawing
    in 1826 (Lister 1988, no. 60); David Blayney
    Brown, however, considers it to be the
    last of three drawings on the same theme
    completed in 1830 (London 1982, pp. 49–50).
    Based on the drawing's similarities to other
    small landscapes in brown wash which
    Palmer is known to have made in 1826, soon
    after moving to Shoreham, the earlier date
    seems more likely.

2   On knowledge of the Nazarenes in London
    in the 1820s, see Vaughan 1979, pp. 20–28
    and 36–38.

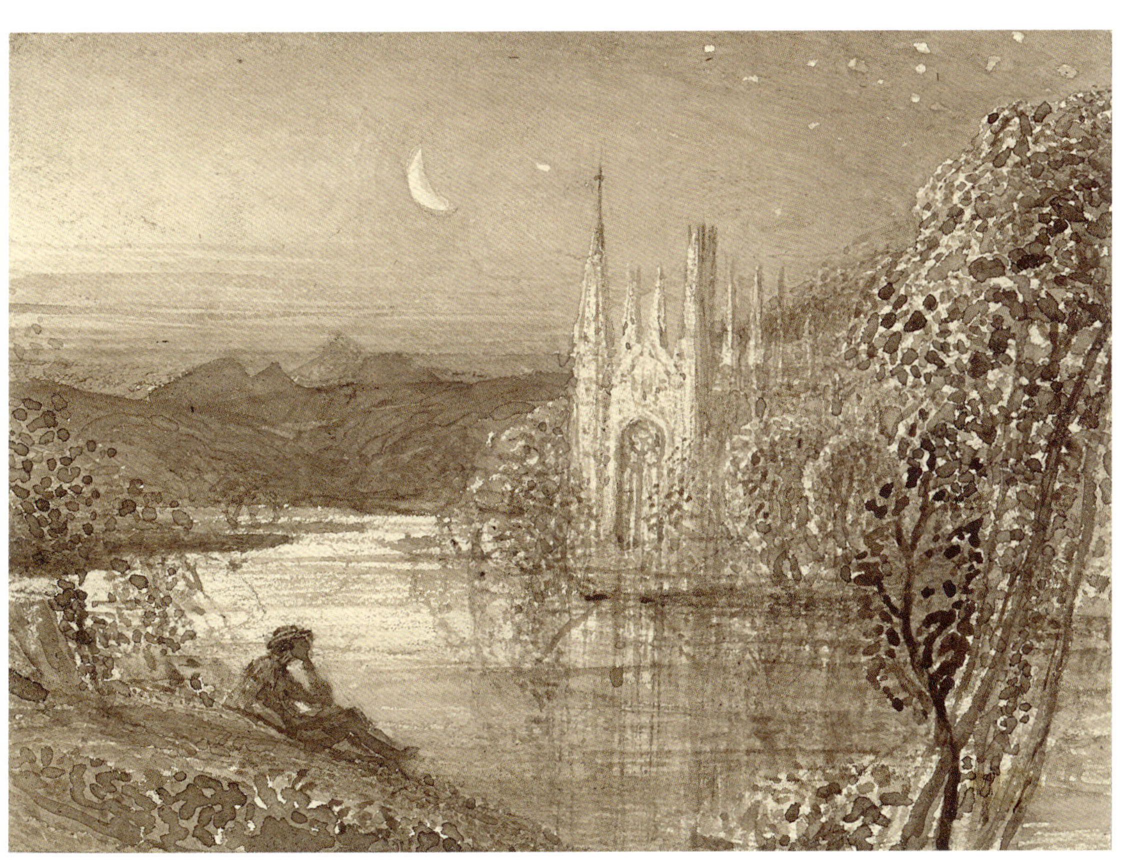

26

FELIX MENDELSSOHN-BARTHOLDY

Hamburg 1809–1847 Leipzig

Sketchbook, 1837–39

The composer Felix Mendelssohn was an enthusiastic amateur draughts-man whose estate contained no fewer than fourteen sketchbooks.[1] Cosmopolitan and widely travelled, he maintained close links with Britain, first visiting in 1829; he performed extensively there, and the Scottish landscape inspired two of his best-known pieces, *The Hebrides* (1830–32) and the *Scottish Symphony* (1829–42). The majority of his surviving sketchbooks record his numerous journeys, beginning in 1822.

The present sketchbook was begun partway through Mendelssohn's honeymoon in April 1837, when he and his wife Cécile travelled from Frankfurt to Mainz, up the Rhine to Freiburg, and then returned to Frankfurt via Heidelberg.[2] Mendelssohn then returned to the sketch-book sporadically in 1839–40. The twenty drawings (two additional leaves, also in the Courtauld collection, have been detached; D.1952.RW.4113 and D.1952.RW.4182) primarily record places visited on the honeymoon journey; with the exception of one of the detached leaves (a watercolour), all of the drawings are done in the pencil that Mendelssohn would have kept in the loops attached to the cover. Several sites carried particular resonance for Romantic artists, such as the views of the Rhine from Sankt Goar and Sankt Goarshausen depicted by Turner twenty years earlier (leaves 12 and 13; see cat. 20). The drawing of the ruined Wernerkirche at Bacharach (leaf 10) is an especially striking example of a favourite motif of Romantic landscapes, executed in painstaking detail in Mendelssohn's slightly naïve hand.

The last drawing in the sketchbook, which is undated, depicts the view from a window of a teahouse on the estate of Mendelssohn's uncle Joseph near Horchheim. The motif of the open window framing a landscape is at the heart of a Romantic conception of the world, symbolic of the meeting of the imagination and nature.[3] The choice of the open window for one of the most highly worked drawings in the sketchbook suggests that while Mendelssohn, like his contemporary Robert Streatfeild (cat. 27), was a dilettante draughtsman, he was very much in tune with the artistic concerns of his time.

Graphite on wove paper, 302 × 232 mm (closed)
The Courtauld Gallery, Samuel Courtauld Trust, D.1952.RW.4100

INSCRIPTIONS

Sites and dates noted on individual drawings by Mendelssohn

PROVENANCE

By descent to Dora Benecke, the artist's granddaughter; presented to Sir Robert Witt, 1949; Witt Bequest, 1952

NOTES

1 Eleven of the sketchbooks are currently held in the Bodleian Library, Oxford (MSS. M. Deneke Mendelssohn c.5, e.3, d.9, d.2, d.15, d.10, d.3, d.11, e.1, d.4 and d.12).
2 The sketchbook has been published, with extensive descriptions of each leaf, in Ward Jones 2011, pp. 181–90.
3 On the motif of the open window in Romanticism, see New York 2011.

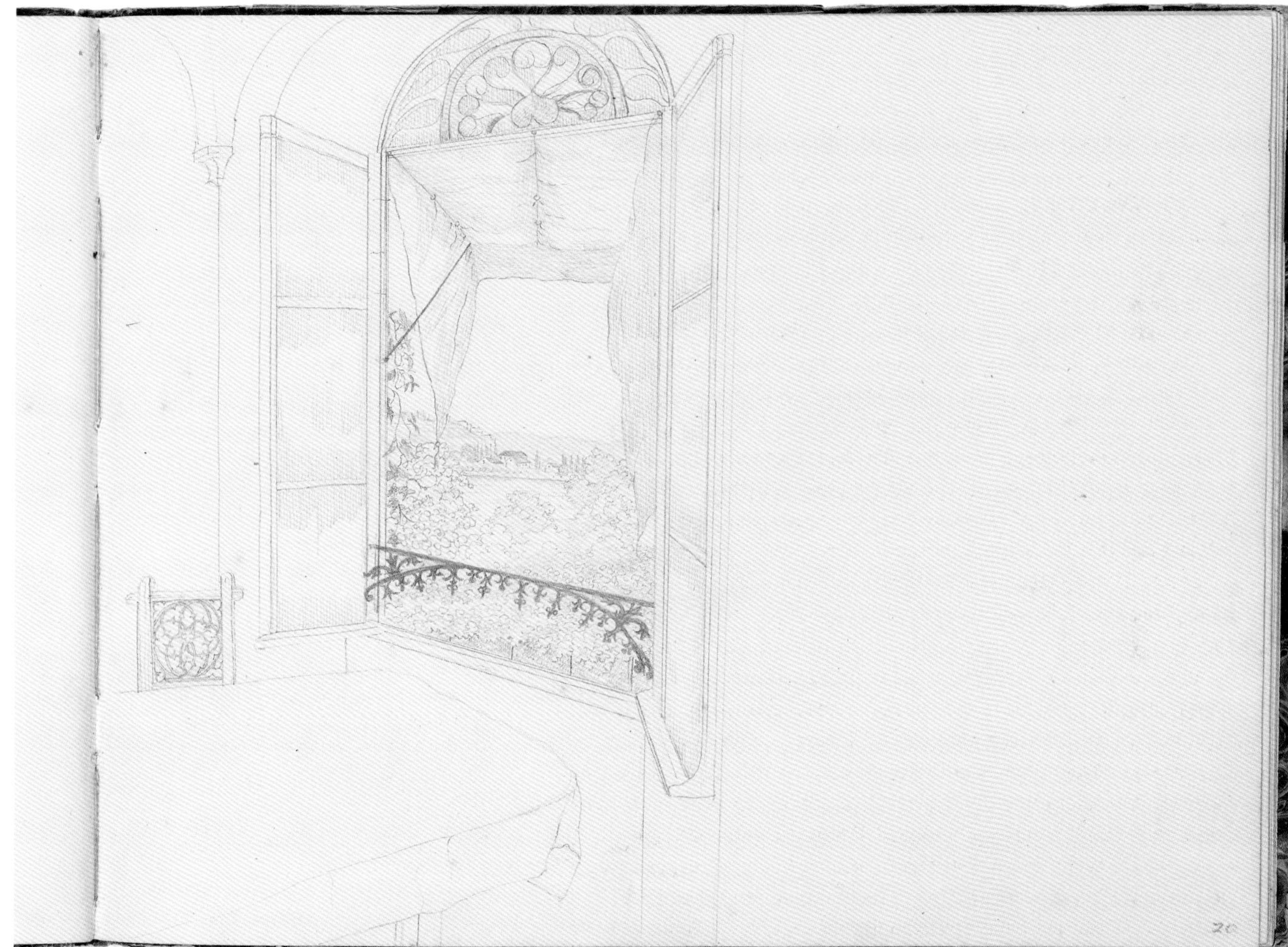

Cowden, near Chiddingstone 1786–1852 Spa

27

Sketchbook, c. 1842

Streatfeild, a British naval officer, retired with the rank of captain in 1815 and began to travel extensively in northern France, Belgium and Germany from the early 1830s. He is likely to have received some tuition in topographical draughtsmanship as part of his officer's training, but this background does not provide a satisfactory explanation for the originality and intensity of the watercolours with which he filled several sketchbooks over the course of his travels.

In 1842, Streatfeild presented an album of his monochrome watercolour drawings to the Grand Duchess Mathilde of Hesse-Darmstadt. The present sketchbook, composed primarily of more highly finished views of the environs of Darmstadt, with 35 drawings in all, appears to be contemporary. Rendered with a fine brush in a restricted palette of blues, greens, browns and greys, the watercolours' exceptionally delicate execution – particularly the sensitive treatment of the trees, not least in a double-page watercolour of a birch grove – and Streatfeild's frequent use of a single figure seen from behind suggest a familiarity with German Romantic landscapes, particularly the work of Friedrich. This *Rückenfigur*, most arrestingly represented in a watercolour where he is shown perched atop a pile of boulders, is typically Romantic, serving both as a point of entry into the landscape for the viewer and a marker of estrangement and isolation. As Matthew Hargraves has noted, Streatfeild's penchant for mining the uncanny in a familiar landscape shows affinities with the writings of Novalis, Coleridge and Wordsworth, all of whom advocated, in the words of the last, "throwing over [the ordinary] a certain colouring of imagination, whereby ordinary things should be presented to the mind in an unusual way".[1]

Watercolour and graphite on wove paper (openings); other media throughout sketchbook; fourteen pencil sketches, 129 × 169 × 13 mm (binding, closed); 123 × 162 mm (leaves)
The Morgan Library & Museum, purchased as the gift of Mrs. Roy O'Connor and Mrs. Sumner Pingree, 1985.60

INSCRIPTIONS

Inside front cover, in pencil, *Darmstadt | & | environs | –* ; inside back cover, in a different hand, several lines in German, French and English, with sketches of two coats of arms, including that of the Odescalchi family, on the adjoining leaf

PROVENANCE

A.G. Lisztein, Zurich

NOTE

1 William Wordsworth, 'Preface', p. 244, cited in New Haven 2010, p. 219.

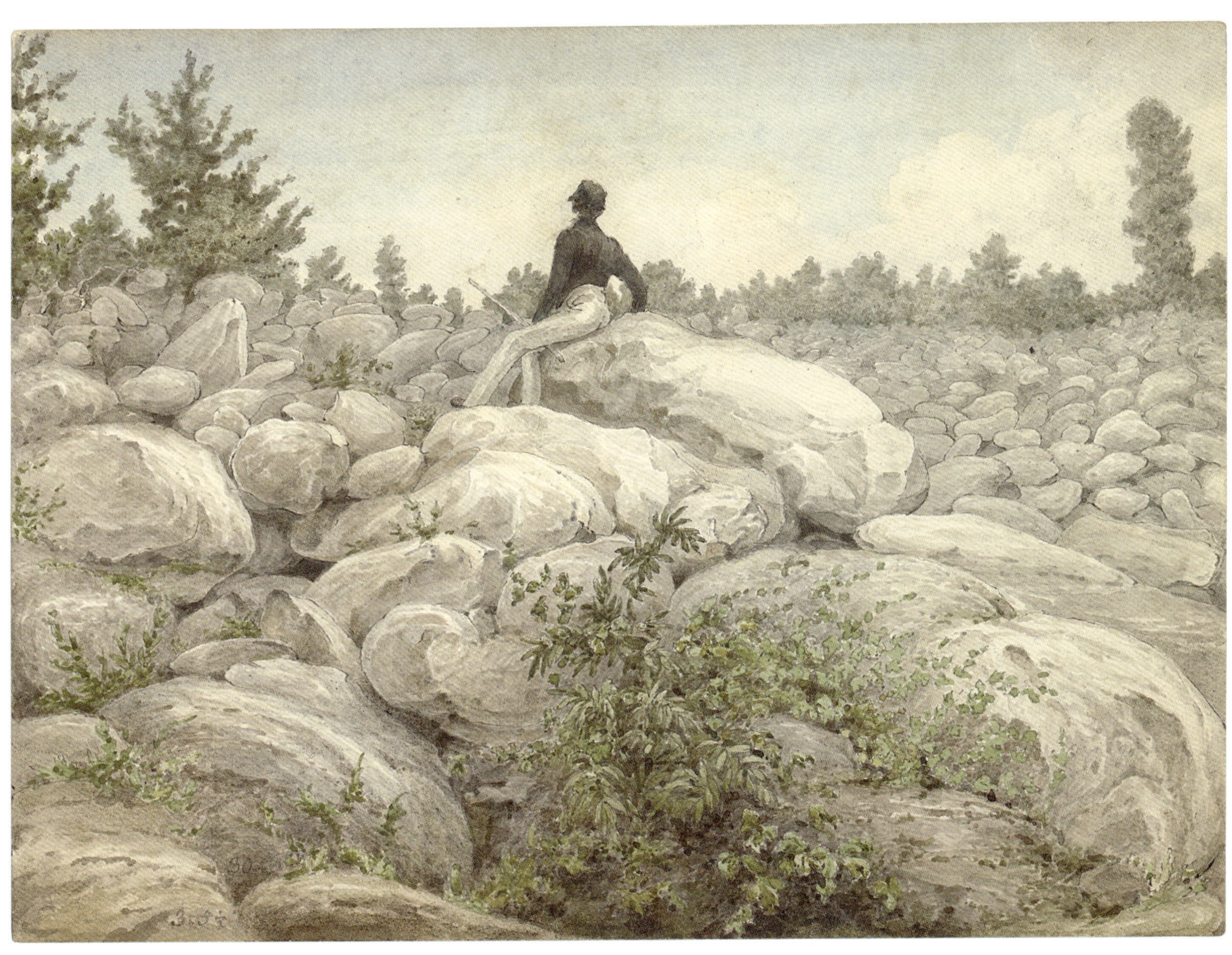

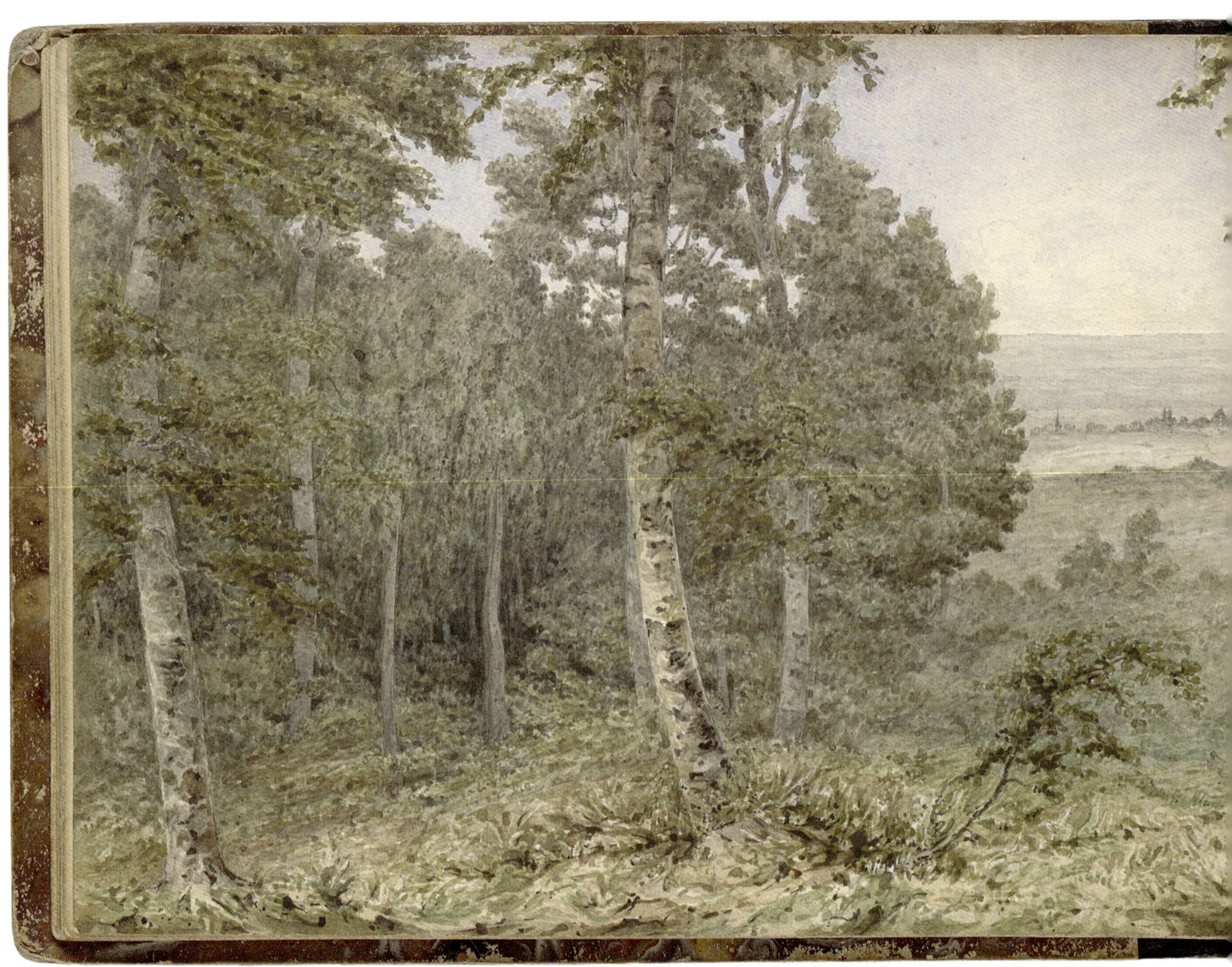

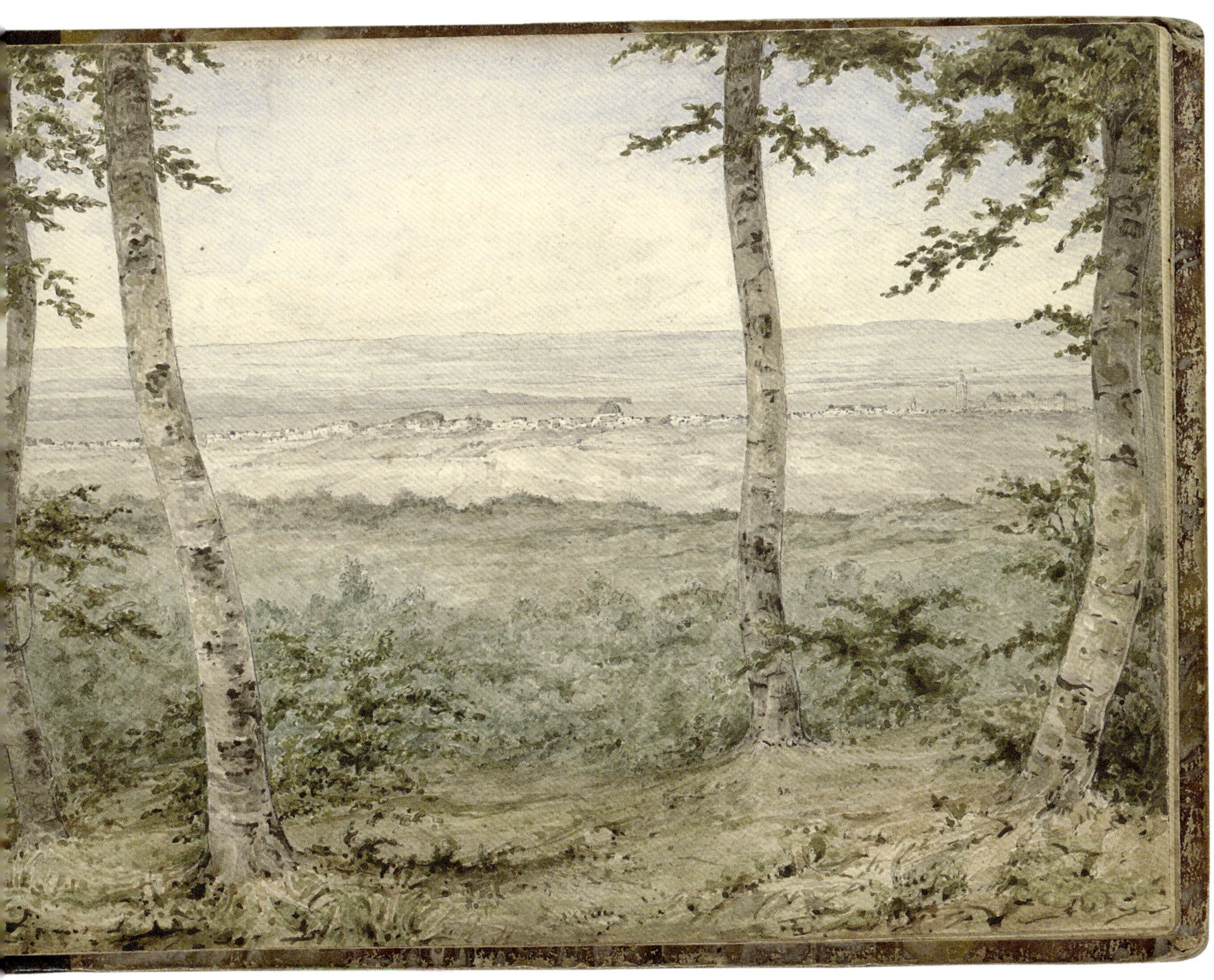

JOSEPH MALLORD WILLIAM TURNER
London 1775–1851 London

Cologne, 1832–33

Turner was commissioned by the publisher John Murray to provide designs for a series of vignettes, to be engraved by Edward Finden, illustrating *The Works of Lord Byron*, in 1831. Rather than illustrations of narrative incidents in Byron's poems, Murray requested topographical images connected to Byron's travels and works.

This watercolour was the design for the title-page vignette of Volume XVI, which included *Don Juan*; it relates to the tenth canto, which describes Don Juan's travels across Central Europe, including a journey along the Rhine narrated in a more flippant tone than the earlier *Childe Harold's Pilgrimage* (Canto X, LXII):

> *From thence he was drawn onwards to Cologne,*
> *A city which presents to the inspector*
> *Eleven thousand maidenheads of bone,*
> *The greatest number flesh hath ever known.*[1]

Using sketches made during his 1817 tour of the Rhine (see cat. 20) as the basis for the design, Turner created an imaginary view, compressing several of the city's principal buildings – the town hall, the tower of Gross Sankt Martin's church and the cathedral – into the small square of the vignette. With the point of a fine brush, he rendered the scene with a delicate, miniaturist touch suitable for reproduction through engraving, limiting his normally broad palette primarily to contrasting shades of blue and red. (Finden's engraving reduced the size of the image still further, with inevitable loss of the finest details.)

In the still-unfinished Cologne Cathedral, which rises like a spectre behind the more solid-looking towers, Turner depicted a potent symbol of the Romantic enthusiasm for the Middle Ages that crossed national borders and ultimately led, in 1842, to the resumption of construction (and completion in 1880). His involvement in the publication of the works of Byron, whose imagination had been equally captured by Germany, underscores the interaction between the visual arts and literature in the transmission of ideas between Britain and Germany.

Watercolour, applied with the point of a fine brush over graphite, on handmade white wove three-ply glazed board (either London or Bristol), 246 × 195 mm (sheet); 144 × 144 mm (image)
The Courtauld Gallery, Samuel Courtauld Trust, D.2007.DS.44

PROVENANCE

William Leech; his sale, Christie's, 21 May 1887, lot 73; Agnew's; Robert Durning Holt, 1887; Sir Edwin Durning Lawrence; T.F. Blackwell; his sale, Christie's, 29 November 1946, lot 68; Mitchell; Christie's, 14 June 1966, lot 179; Daly; Christie's, 21 November 1978, lot 80; Leger Galleries; R.A. Shuck, 1979; Leger Galleries, 1984; Dorothy Scharf (1942–2004), 1985; Scharf Bequest, 2007

NOTE

1 The "eleven thousand maidenheads of bone" alludes to the legend of Saint Ursula and the eleven thousand virgins martyred with her in Cologne.

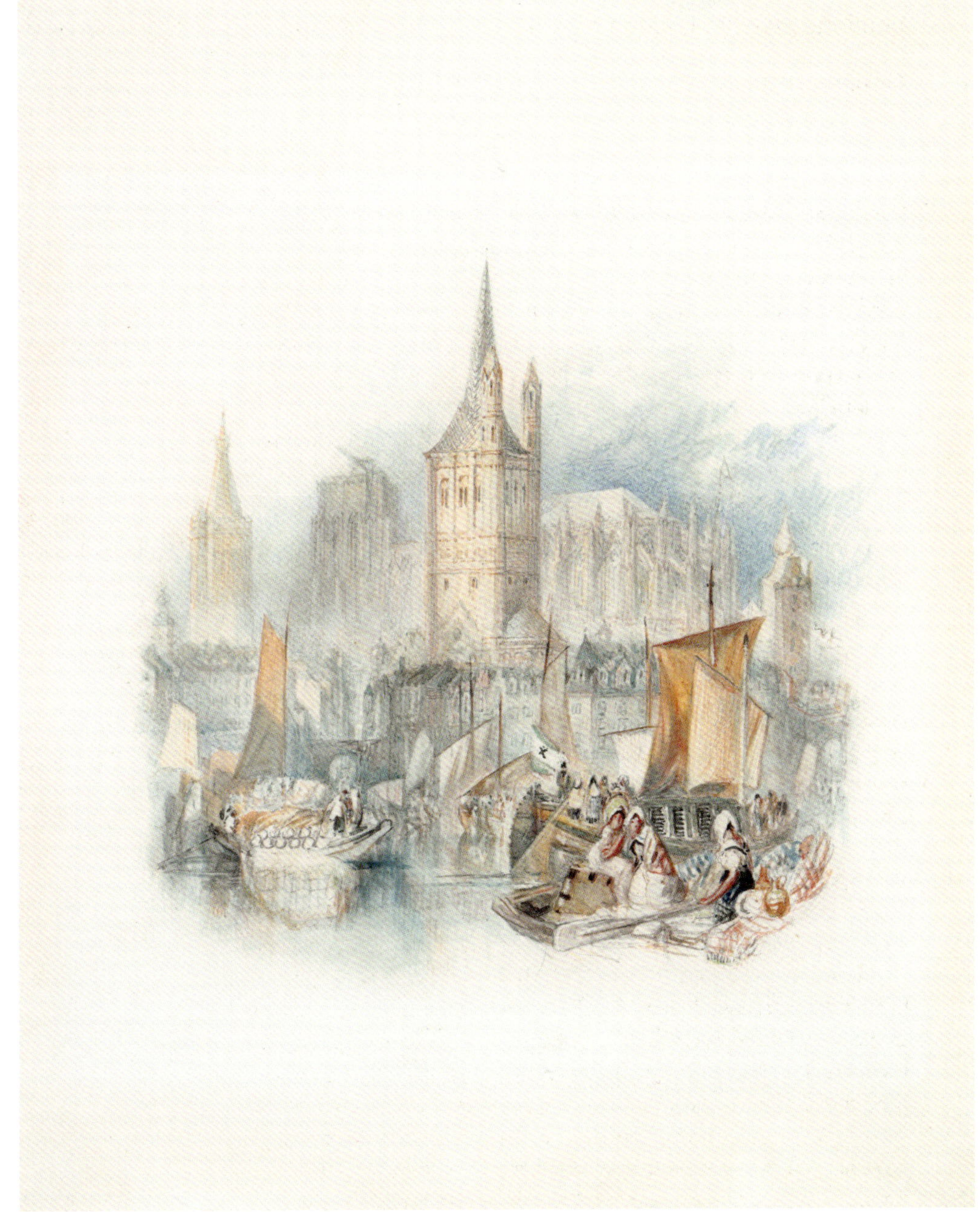

WORKS CITED

BOOKS AND ARTICLES

Alpers 1983
Svetlana Alpers, *The Art of Describing: Dutch Art in the Seventeenth Century*, Chicago, 1983

Beckett 1962–68
R. B. Beckett, ed., *John Constable's Correspondence*, Ipswich, 1962–68

Belsey 2008
Hugh Belsey, 'Drawings by Gainsborough: Supplement', *Master Drawings* XLVI, no. 4, 2008

Börsch-Supan 1960
Helmut Börsch-Supan, 'Die Bildgestaltung bei Caspar David Friedrich', Ph.D. diss., Munich, 1960

Börsch-Supan and Jähnig 1973
Helmut Börsch-Supan and Karl Wilhelm Jähnig, *Caspar David Friedrich. Gemälde, Druckgraphik und bildmässige Zeichnungen*, Munich, 1973

Carus 2002
Carl Gustav Carus, *Nine Letters on Painting*, trans. David Britt, Los Angeles, 2002

Cook and Wedderburn 1904
E.T. Cook and Alexander Wedderburn, eds., *The Works of John Ruskin*, vol. 6, London, 1904

Cozens 1786
Alexander Cozens, *A New Method of Assisting the Invention of Drawing Original Compositions of Landscape*, London, 1786

Eastlake 1967 (1840)
Charles Lock Eastlake, trans., *Goethe's Theory of Colours*, London, 1967 (first published 1840)

Farington 1978–84
Joseph Farington, *The Diary of Joseph Farington*, ed. Kenneth Garlick and Angus Macintyre (vols. 1–6) and Kathryn Cave (vols. 7–14), New Haven and London, 1978–84

Gage 1969
John Gage, *Colour in Turner*, London, 1969

Gage 1980
John Gage, *Goethe on Art*, Berkeley, 1980

Girtin and Loshak 1954
Thomas Girtin and David Loshak, *The Art of Thomas Girtin*, London, 1954

Grummt 2011
Christina Grummt, *Caspar David Friedrich. Die Zeichnungen*, 2 vols., Munich, 2011

Hardie 1966
Martin Hardie, *Watercolour Painting in Britain, Vol. 1: The Eighteenth Century*, London, 1966

Hayes 1983
John Hayes, 'Gainsborough Drawings: A Supplement to the Catalogue Raisonné', *Master Drawings*, XXI, no. 4, 1983, pp. 367–91

Hayes 2001
John Hayes, ed., *The Letters of Thomas Gainsborough*, New Haven, 2001

Hill 2003
David Hill, 'J.M.W. Turner: from the world to art and back again', *Turner Society News*, 95, December 2003, pp. 8–16

Honour 1979
Hugh Honour, *Romanticism*, Boulder, 1979

Koerner 2009
Joseph Leo Koerner, *Caspar David Friedrich and the subject of landscape*, London, 2009 (first published 1990)

Lenz 1989
Christian Lenz, *The Neue Pinakothek, Munich*, London, 1989

Leslie 1843
C.R. Leslie, *Memoirs of the Life of John Constable, Esq. R.A.*, London, 1843

Lister 1974
Raymond Lister, ed., *The Letters of Samuel Palmer*, Oxford, 1974

Lister 1988
Raymond Lister, *Catalogue Raisonné of the Works of Samuel Palmer*, Cambridge, 1988

Oppé 1952
A.P. Oppé, *Alexander and John Robert Cozens*, London, 1952

Palmer 1974
A.H. Palmer, *The Life and Letters of Samuel Palmer*, London, 1974

Reusch 1999
Johann J.K. Reusch, 'Caspar David Friedrich and national antiquarianism in Northern Germany', in Martin Myrone and Lucy Peltz, eds., *Producing the Past: Aspects of antiquarian culture and practice, 1700–1850*, Aldershot, 1999, pp. 95–114

Reynolds 1984
Graham Reynolds, *The Later Paintings and Drawings of John Constable*, New Haven and London, 1984

Schiff 1988
Gert Schiff, ed., *German Essays on Art History*, New York, 1988

Schönle 2000
Andreas Schönle, *Authenticity and Fiction in the Russian Literary Journey, 1790–1840*, Cambridge, MA, 2000

Vaughan 1979
William Vaughan, *German Romanticism and English Art*, New Haven and London, 1979

Vaughan 1994
William Vaughan, *German Romantic Painting*, 2nd edition, New Haven, 1994

Ward Jones 2011
Peter Ward Jones, 'A Mendelssohn drawing book and other documents in the Courtauld Institute of Art, London', *Mendelssohn Studien*, vol. 17, 2011, pp. 181–90

Wolf-Timm 1991
Telse Wolf-Timm, *Theodor Rehbenitz, 1791–1861: Persönlichkeit und Werk*, Kiel, 1991

EXHIBITION CATALOGUES

Cologne 1986
Uwe Westfehling, *Meisterzeichnungen von Leonardo bis zu Rodin. Eine Auswahl von Miniaturen, Handzeichnungen aus der Graphischen Sammlung*, Wallraf-Richartz-Museum, Cologne, 1986

Edinburgh 2000
Edward Morris, ed., *Constable's Clouds*, National Galleries of Scotland, Edinburgh, 2000

Hamburg 2002
Wolkenstudien/Cloud Studies: Johann Georg von Dillis, Thomas Le Claire Kunsthandel, Hamburg, 2002

London 1972
William Vaughan, *Caspar David Friedrich 1774–1840: Romantic Landscape Painting in Dresden*, Tate Gallery, London, 1972

London 1982
David Blayney Brown, *Samuel Palmer, 1805–1881: Loan Exhibition from the Ashmolean Museum Oxford*, Hazlitt, Gooden & Fox, London, 1982

London 1994
Cecilia Powell, *Turner in Germany*, Tate Gallery, London, 1994

London 1997
Timothy Wilcox, *Francis Towne*, Tate Gallery, London, 1997

London 2005
William Vaughan, Elizabeth Barker and Colin Harrison, *Samuel Palmer 1805–1881: Vision and Landscape*, British Museum, London, 2005

London 2008
Joanna Selborne, ed., *Paths to Fame: Turner Watercolours from The Courtauld Gallery*, Courtauld Gallery, London, 2008

Madrid 2009
Christina Grummt, ed., *Caspar David Friedrich: The Art of Drawing*, Fundación Juan March, Madrid, 2009

Munich 1991
Christoph Heilmann, *Johann Georg von Dillis (1759–1841). Landschaft und Menschenbild*, Bayerische Staatsgemäldesammlungen München, Neue Pinakothek, Munich, 1991

New Haven 1980
Andrew Wilton, *The Art of Alexander and John Robert Cozens*, Yale Center for British Art, New Haven, 1980

New Haven 2007
Matthew Hargraves, *Great British Watercolors from the Paul Mellon Collection*, Yale Center for British Art, New Haven, 2007

New Haven 2010
Matthew Hargraves, *Varieties of Romantic Experience*, Yale Center for British Art, New Haven, 2010

New York 2001
Sabine Rewald, ed., *Moonwatchers*, Metropolitan Museum of Art, New York, 2001

New York 2011
Sabine Rewald, ed., *Rooms with a View: The Open Window in the Nineteenth Century*, Metropolitan Museum of Art, New York, 2011

Weimar and Hamburg 2008
Hubertus Gassner and Ernst-Gerhard Güse, eds., *Jakob Philipp Hackert. Europas Landschaftsmaler der Goethezeit*, Klassik Stiftung, Weimar, and Hamburger Kunsthalle, 2008